Spirit of a Native Place

THE NATIONAL MUSEUM OF THE AMERICAN INDIAN opened on September 21, 2004.

KIOWA CAMP, 1895. *Fort Sill, Oklahoma.* P13141

WEDDING DANCE, 1998. *Río Copalita, Mexico.*

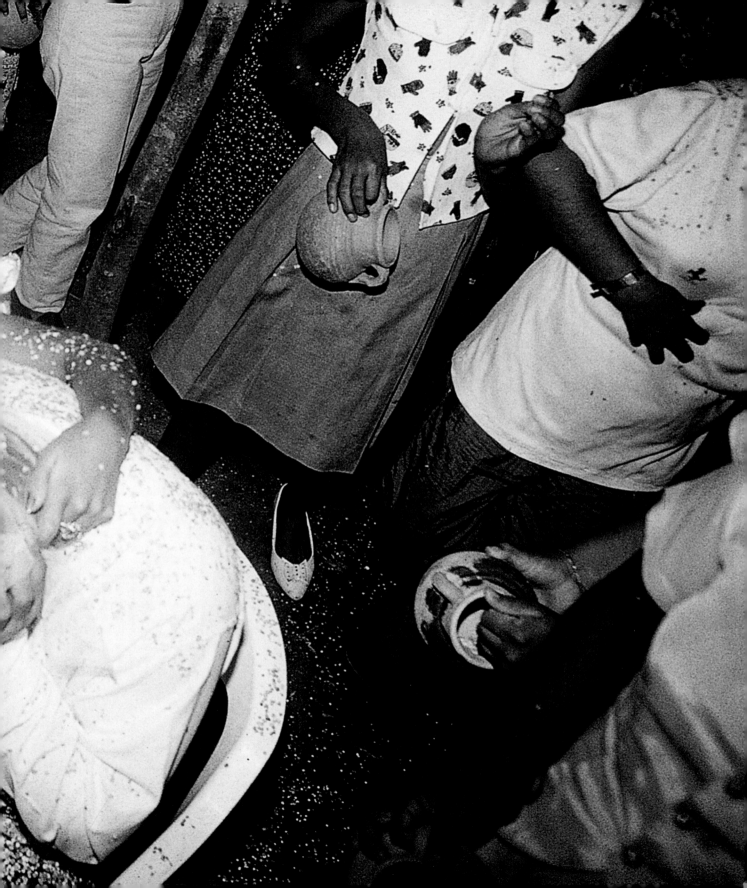

WELCOMING GUESTS during the Feast of San Pedro, 2000. *San Pedro Huamelula, Mexico.*

YUPIK ESKIMOS traveling from Stebbins to Kotlick for the Messenger Feast, 2003. *Alaska*.

FIREWORKS ON the fourth Friday of Lent, 1998. *Santa María Huatulco, Mexico.*

Spirit of a Native Place

BUILDING THE NATIONAL MUSEUM OF THE AMERICAN INDIAN

DUANE BLUE SPRUCE, EDITOR

NATIONAL MUSEUM OF THE AMERICAN INDIAN, SMITHSONIAN INSTITUTION

IN ASSOCIATION WITH

 NATIONAL GEOGRAPHIC

WASHINGTON, D.C.

Contents

An Honor and a Privilege

by Duane Blue Spruce

In the past, Rick West, Founding Director of the National Museum of the American Indian (NMAI), has written the eloquent Forewords that grace the museum's books. For this book, however, Rick has contributed an evocative, personal essay tracing the path that led him to this place, and the experiences that shaped his vision of the museum. So the enjoyable responsibility of writing this text has fallen to me.

There is a certain logic to my selection: over the years I've often been called upon to act as Rick's representative on design and construction issues for the museum on the National Mall, and as a result, I serve as a reasonable institutional memory. As a Native American and an architect, I am honored to work for the museum and to be a part of its development. I know that my experiences here represent the greatest job I'll ever have. It may be a cliché, but, for me, building the museum can best be described as a journey. It is a journey that has taken me to beautiful places, enabled me to meet many wonderful people, and brought me memories and relationships that will be with me forever.

LIGHT STREAMS through the museum's unfinished prism window during construction.

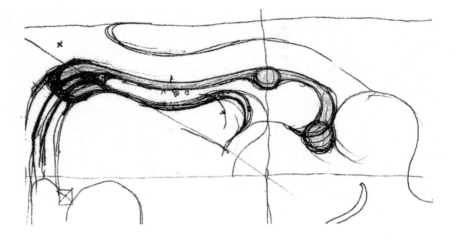

EARLY SKETCHES by architect Douglas Cardinal illustrate important themes in the design of the museum on the National Mall, including the building's curvilinear form and orientation along an east-west axis.

My journey began in March 1993, when I was asked to take part in a two-day design workshop conducted by the Smithsonian and the architectural team assigned to design the museum's Cultural Resources Center, which opened in Washington's Maryland suburbs five years later. At the time, I was working at the Institute of American Indian Arts, a museum and college of the creative arts in Santa Fe. The workshop took place in the gym on the nearby campus of the Santa Fe Indian School, the Pueblo high school where my grandfather taught wood shop for more than twenty-five years and where my father and his brother and sister were raised. It was exciting to meet so many talented Native and non-Native design professionals at the workshop, and to observe the commonalities among the major design ideas that were presented. A few months later, NMAI offered me a position. My wife, Ida—pregnant with our first child—our neurotic cat, and I left the blue skies of the Southwest and drove across the country straight into the heat and humidity of a Washington summer.

In the first weeks after we moved, I met fellow staff and familiarized myself with the museum's existing facilities—the George Gustav Heye Center in lower Manhattan, which was preparing for its opening in October

1994, and the Research Branch in the Bronx. When I was a boy growing
up on Staten Island, my mother took me to the Museum of the American
Indian (MAI) on 155th Street, our predecessor institution, but I had never
been to MAI's Bronx site. Chapter 4 of this book, especially the photographs on pages 122–126, offers a glimpse of what the Research Branch
was like. Getting off the elevator, I was greeted by a wall of pottery from
Chaco Canyon, objects arranged four or five rows deep on floor-to-ceiling
shelves. I was awestruck by the incredible beauty and sheer numbers of
these artifacts. Although these objects had been created by my ancestors,
until then I had seen them only in books.

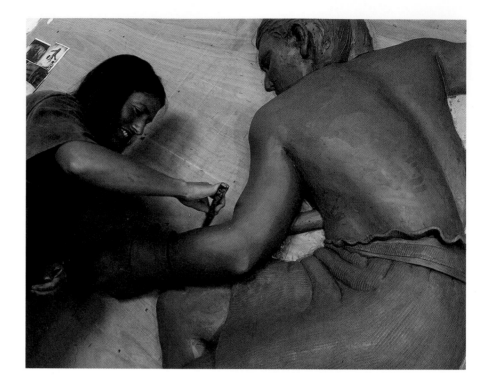

That moment, when I stepped off an elevator and into the Pueblo past, marked my entry into NMAI's world. If I were to add that day, faintly, to the timeline of the early history of the museum, it would come after NMAI's extensive consultations with Native communities about what they wanted the new museum to be, but in time for me to be an advocate for the remarkable architectural program based on their vision—the museum's landmark working document, entitled *The Way of the People.* That day would be followed by more conspicuous notations of endless design meetings, presentations, and reviews. There were not only dozens of design consultants on a project of this scale, but the Smithsonian—the client—had an equal number of representatives and stakeholders who weighed in on everything from the sound transmission of the mechanical ductwork to the operation of the door hardware. To offer a variation of a Woody Allen line, there are things worse than death; anyone who has attended a day-long hardware meeting knows exactly what I'm talking about.

Although I didn't take part in the early community consultations, I regard them, in some ways, as the most creative period in the museum's development. The discussions reached beyond the design of the building to explore how people hoped visitors would experience the museum. A series of themes emerged. One is that the museum should strive to honor the natural world in all its aspects. Another is that the architecture should make specific references to Native beliefs. Everyone also thought it was essential for the museum to show that Native cultures are very much alive today, to help sustain Native languages, and to cultivate strong relationships with contemporary Native communities.

The Way of the People has proved a remarkably insightful and resilient document. Some participants addressed the overall design of the building and grounds:

Make it a place in the wilderness, with large natural rocks, wild plants, trees, herbs, water over rocks.

In Central and South America, our monuments are natural elements.

Others described the feeling we should strive to convey:

A living museum, not formal and quiet.

Focus on creativity, rather than new versus old.

Hospitality is one thing you will always find among Native Americans, and hopefully always will. It was our first downfall.

Adaptability and survival: how can we portray that inner strength?

Some people stressed the symbolism of the museum and our responsibility to Native America:

An Indian child has to come here and be proud. We have nothing here in this capital.

If the museum can do anything, it is to help prevent us from getting to a point where we have to go to a museum to learn about ourselves.

ROXANNE SWENTZELL (Santa Clara Pueblo) created the series of bronze figures and ceramic masks mounted outside the theater on the first floor. The Pueblo rain dancer she is shown modeling is a symbol of the forces that nourish life and a nod to the many dancers who will perform in the theater over the years.

TLINGIT MASTER-CARVER

Nathan Jackson, working in his studio in Ketchikan, Alaska, sculpted the twenty-foot totem pole that stands beside the museum's monumental staircase.

Others reminded us of our limitations:

My grandparents were my collection, my museum. The museum shouldn't mean a loss of community and family.

Programs that reach Indian communities are more important than buildings.

Many of the suggestions were specific:

Reflect the solar calendar and equinoxes in the design, not just as symbols, but in actual use.

Skylights could be used to give a sense of the sky.

Fire in the middle is important as the spiritual center of the house.

For Inuit people, a dome—not all squares, but roundness.

Some contradicted each other:

Some tribes would want entry from the east, the sunrise.

Our door [in southeast Alaska] has to face the beach.

(Actually, the museum entrance manages to face the sunrise and the beach, one advantage to being on the East Coast.)

Some of the statements were cautionary:

Diversity and conflict should not be watered down.

A reverence for things like planting corn and beans is important, but don't make us out to be the spiritual gurus of the world.

I've never seen a tipi made out of other materials that looked good.

Some were protective:

The ground should be blessed before construction.

And some didn't make it to the final design:

My Northwest people would want a salmon pit outside the museum.
I see the limitations of the Mall. Tint the building purple!

The vision session and design workshop that followed further refined our understanding of what the museum should be. As the conceptual design took shape, staff members continued to venture from New York and Washington, to hear new ideas and to enlist support for the project.

We visited the wonderful cultural center on the Makah Reservation in Neah Bay, Washington. Among the many things that stay in my mind from that visit is the staff's resourceful use of large metal baking trays to store artifacts in metal shelving units.

Douglas Cardinal (Blackfoot), a key member of the original architectural team, arranged for us to tour his Canadian Museum of Civilization in Ottawa. It was a beautiful sunny day, and Douglas brought us to the museum by boat. The vantage point from the Ottawa River afforded stunning views of the building, and I had a greater appreciation for the strength of Douglas's design and its masterful relationship to its setting beside the river and to Parliament on the opposite shore. Douglas, standing at the helm of the boat in his bare feet, reveled in the experience of his creation.

People working on what we called the Exhibit Master Plan visited tribal museums and community cultural centers for inspiration. On a single trip to Wyoming and Montana, we stopped at the Buffalo Bill Historical Center in Cody, the Shoshone Tribal Cultural Center and Sacagawea's memorial at Fort Washakie, the Wind River petroglyphs, the Little Bighorn Battlefield, and the community museum and Arapaho mission in Ethete. At a lunch hosted by the Arapaho community, we were reminded of the tremendous generosity found throughout Indian Country, and of our mandate to bring that quality into the museum.

In Monroe, North Carolina, a local nursery had been contracted to

NATIVE BUILDINGS and monuments, as well as Native symbolism and natural rock formations, influenced the museum's design. The building's low, stepped dome evokes the step pyramids of the pre-Columbian Americas. Temple of the Sun. *Teotihuacán, Mexico. N23171*

THE KASOTA STONE cladding on the building presented a major challenge to stone cutters and masons. The design includes convex and concave curves with more than fifty different radii. More than 2,400 tons of split-face stone, the primary stone finish used on the exterior walls, were produced for the project. Vetter Stone estimates that, all told, the building required more than 50,000 pieces of cut stone.

provide many of the plants to landscape our site on the Mall. I remember the puzzled look on the motel attendant's face as each member of our traveling party, checking in late at night, requested a wake-up call for four o'clock the next morning. What better way to show respect for the plants and those who would be caring for them than to join with representatives of the nearby Cherokee, Lumbee, and Choctaw communities for a sunrise blessing ceremony? Blessing ceremonies were held at nurseries in Connecticut and Pennsylvania, as well.

At a quarry near Alma, Quebec, we met with the chief and representatives of the Montagnais people of Mashteuiatsh to bless the boulders, or Grandfather Rocks, that are the elders of our landscape, and to wish the stones a safe journey to Washington. At the Mashteuiatsh Amerindian Museum, Thelesh, a woman from the community, gave us a demonstration of making artistic patterns on birch bark with her teeth. She had learned this almost-lost art as a child. Her family was camping in the forest one night when it began to storm. Her mother sought to calm Thelesh's fears by teaching her to decorate bark. At one of the quarry sites, the design team's ethnobotanist, Donna House (Navajo/Oneida), gathered the French Canadian quarry workers together and explained the importance of the boulders before distributing corn pollen and offering a prayer for the group. I try to imagine what those guys told their families when they went home that evening; I hope it was that they'd had an unusually good day.

In Martha's Vineyard, Massachusetts, we visited Berta Welch (Wampanoag) and her husband, Vernon Giles, the couple who created the inlaid shell work that decorates the museum shops. Berta and Vern took the time to show us the process from beginning to end. They go out on a boat and harvest Quahog shells from the bottom of a pond with a rusty, rake-like tool; split the clams open and clean them, giving the meat to family and friends; then cut, grind, and polish the tiles—a extraordinarily labor-intensive

process fully justified by the beauty of the end product. Over a delicious homemade feast of lobster and other seafood, Berta introduced us to the rest of her family, all of whom would help make the inlay for the museum.

At Pipestone National Monument in Minnesota, we visited Travis Erickson (Sisseton Wahpeton Sioux), who made the pipes displayed in the museum's Lelawi Theater. Park Service regulations prohibit the use of power tools at the national monument, so Travis quarries the stone by hand, using a wedge, a sledgehammer, his strength, and his keen knowledge. He feels a deep spiritual connection to the stone and to his craft. To watch him quarry his way down through eighteen-feet of quartzite to reach the layer of pipestone was to see a true craftsman at work.

Not all our visits were to beautiful places in Indian Country. In a loft in downtown Manhattan, the design team met with artist Charles Ross to discuss the fabrication and installation of the prism window in the south wall of the Potomac, the museum's soaring rotunda. Charles dazzled us with his artistic precision and his technical knowledge of physics and astronomy.

In Kansas City, Missouri, we visited the A. Zahner Company, the architectural metal shop that fabricated the exquisite copper screen wall that surrounds the Potomac, bringing an artistic vision into reality with great skill. The Zahner staff's imagination is evidenced by their use of a bowling ball fastened to the end of a metal rod to pound dimples into the surface of the copper.

In Mankato, Minnesota, a group visited the Vetter Stone Company, suppliers of the beautiful Kasota stone that covers most of the museum's exterior. A company that has been in the Vetter family for decades, Vetter uses both early twentieth-century belt-driven stonecutting equipment and state-of-the-art equipment from Italy. Initially, its engineers and stonefitters were not certain how to cut Kasota stone into the curved cladding of the museum. But by the time of our visit, they had adapted their machinery and mastered the necessary technique.

There were many surprising moments. Often during the conceptual design phase of the project, we would invite members of Native nations, and other friends of the museum, to regional meetings to comment on the architecture. At one of these sessions, in a hotel conference room in Minneapolis, a group of tough-looking men wearing biker gear sat together at one table. They listened to our presentation and to everyone else's comments in intimidating silence. Then, as the meeting neared its end, one of them stood up and said, "Our tribe is matrilineal, and our mothers, wives, sisters, and daughters are held in high esteem. We just want to commend you and thank you for building the first female building on the Mall."

ON MARTHA'S VINEYARD, Vernon Giles (opposite) harvests quahog clams. At their workshop in Martha's Vineyard, Vernon and his wife Berta Welch (Wampanoag) converted bushels of shells into the tiles that decorate the cabinetry of the Museum Shops.

Now our travels have come full circle, and the people who welcomed me and my colleagues into their communities years ago are coming to Washington to put the finishing touches on their contributions to the museum and to celebrate its opening. The Native Hawaiians who graciously provided us with the volcanic rock that orients the building to the west recently held a ceremony to bless their stone. Then they visited the other cardinal direction markers to drape them with leis made of maile leaves, an honor traditionally reserved for important, happy occasions.

Since we came to Washington, my wife and I have been blessed with the births of our two children, Miles and Milena. It makes me inordinately proud to hear my children refer to the building as "Daddy's museum." More than ten years into fatherhood—ten years that coincide with my work at the museum—I am keenly aware of the cultural legacy this project leaves for future generations.

I hope the essays in this book convey a sense of what the museum's creation means to a few of the people who have been privileged to take part in it. In his Introduction, George Horse Capture, senior counselor to the director of NMAI, remembers what it was like to be a part of the first consultations, when the creative groundwork for the museum was laid. Rick West (Southern Cheyenne) writes about his Oklahoma boyhood, and about the importance of Indians' having a place on the National Mall. Architect Johnpaul Jones (Cherokee/Choctaw), Donna House, and textile artist Ramona Sakiestewa (Hopi)—with Douglas Cardinal, the individuals most responsible for the marvelous architecture, rich surrounding habitat, and beautiful interior design of the museum—describe how they went about their creative collaboration.

Mary Jane Lenz, a curator at the Museum of the American Indian as well as NMAI, profiles George Gustav Heye, the New York businessman who, over the course of six decades, assembled the most comprehensive collection of Native North, Central, and South American cultural material in the world. John Haworth (Cherokee), director of the George Gustav Heye Center, contributes an essay on a few of the contributions Indians have made to the culture of New York City. Liz Hill (Red Lake Band of Chippewa) follows the museum's collections from their longtime home in the Bronx to NMAI's state-of-the-art Cultural Resources Center in Maryland. Finally, NMAI Deputy Director Doug Evelyn gives a brief history of the museum's site on the National Mall, from its once-Native past to its new, Native present.

THE DEACON Jeffers family (Wampanoag), ca. 1900. *Gay Head, Massachusetts. N15814*

INTRODUCTION

The Way of the People

by George Horse Capture

The creation of the National Museum of the American Indian represents a significant contribution to educating the world about the ways of Indian people. As a curator and historian who has had the honor of being a small part of this effort, I believe that to appreciate fully the importance of this moment, we must take a brief look at Indian history.

The population of the Western Hemisphere before 1492 remains a subject of research and debate. Recent studies, however, estimate that 500 years ago more than five million people lived in what is now the lower forty-eight United States. Soon after the invasion from Europe, confrontations between the newcomers and the ancient Native inhabitants broke out, and within a short time it became apparent that foreign technology would overcome the Indian people. Entire tribes were destroyed. Our forebears who survived saw their lands taken, their religions and languages forbidden. By 1900, barely 250,000 Native Americans remained, and our ways seemed doomed to disappear.

MOTHER AND DAUGHTER Bernice Begay (Navajo) and Bah Chee (Navajo), 1981. *Jeddito Island, Arizona. P23390*

But we did not disappear. With the closing of the frontier, the pressure on tribes—no longer seen as obstacles to national expansion—eased, and the death rate among Native people stabilized. In the first decade of the twentieth century, more Indian people were born than died, reversing a trend that began with the landing of Columbus. Our spirit had refused to succumb, and, bruised and battered, we embarked on a new century, full of hope.

Indian leaders recognized that in order to endure, we would have to gather together, establish priorities for survival, muster our strength and pride, work toward asserting our interests, and march toward the future. And we did, slowly at first, learning new ways, taking our struggle to the courts, including, increasingly, the court of public opinion. In 1924 we gained the right to vote. Warriors volunteered for service in the two world wars. Returning home victorious, some Indian veterans moved their families off the desolate reservations to the cities, seeking a share in the American dream.

Each of these successes marked a step toward our regaining a place in the world. In 1969, when a small group of college students occupied the abandoned island prison of Alcatraz, in San Francisco Bay, offering to purchase it from the U.S. government for twenty-four dollars in beads and red cloth, the modern Indian civil rights movement was born. Many positive things resulted from that event, but perhaps the most important and far-reaching was that we became committed to making sweeping improvements in our own lives. Indian students pursued college degrees as never before. Indian pride blossomed.

I speak here as more than a curator and historian. After growing up on the Fort Belknap Reservation in Montana, I joined the Navy, then settled in the Bay area. In 1969 I was doing what even then I recognized as my assimilation gig, settling into white society as a civil servant working for

IROQUOIS FOOTBALL team, ca. 1900.

Onondaga Reservation, New York.

P15305

NANTICOKE FISHERMEN,

ca. 1911.

Delaware. N12637

the state of California. Then Alcatraz happened. I quit my job, grabbed a sleeping bag, and joined the protest. I spent the first night in the part of the prison that had been death row, alone with my thoughts, far from the drumming and celebrating. When the occupation ended, I applied to the University of California at Berkeley, received a scholarship, and took every course I could find that touched even remotely on Indian affairs. Alcatraz was a beacon that awakened us and set us on a new course. It taught us that we were Indians.

While I was at Alcatraz, my friend and colleague Rick West was at Stanford Law School, just down the California coast. And I flatter myself that it is no coincidence that when Rick was named the first director of the National Museum of the American Indian, he embarked upon a course of action unheard of then in the museum world. In a peaceful yet profound revolution, Rick and his associates realized that the only proper way to create a museum representative of Native people was to hear from those people themselves. At the same time, the act of consulting with Native communities would let the people there know that their experiences and ideas would not only be recognized in the new museum, they would guide its conception.

The legislation establishing the National Museum of the American Indian called for the creation of three facilities: a gallery and program space in New York City, now the George Gustav Heye Center; a home for the collections on Smithsonian property in the Maryland suburbs of Washington, the Cultural Resources Center; and the museum on the National Mall. After preliminary sessions in Sulphur, Oklahoma, and Warm Springs, Oregon, in 1990, and a brief series of meetings the next year in Washington with Native and non-Native museum directors, designers, artists, researchers, educators, archivists, and experts in technology, the museum staff and its consultants traveled to New York

UMATILLA PEOPLE in front of a house covered with reed mats. *Umatilla Reservation, Oregon.* *P9313*

SPIRIT OF A NATIVE PLACE

City, Santa Fe, Oklahoma City, Anchorage, Billings, and other sites to learn how people there envisioned the museum. Surveys also played an important part in gathering ideas from Indian communities, as did visits by museum staff to reservations to speak with spiritual leaders and elders.

As one of a small group of American Indian museum professionals, I joined the project to help facilitate these community consultations. The artist Rina Swentzell (Tewa/Santa Clara Pueblo) and the writer and photographer Rick Hill (Tuscarora) played the same role. Enthralled as I was with the developing museum, the meetings in themselves were a great joy. The achievements and diversity of the Native participants spoke to the thoroughness of the selection process. Even then I had been in the Indian business for many, many moons. I thought I knew, or had at least heard of, most of the key players—and indeed I did see many people I expected to see—but there were many other accomplished Indian participants whose names and faces were new to me.

The first few minutes before the prayer that began each meeting were taken up with handshakes, hugs, and backslaps as we all greeted one another, old comrades in arms reunited on a new mission. We were filled with joy and hope for our new adventure. Later, after a long and exhausting day, we would get together and visit, catching up on the moccasin gossip. It was a grand time and a rewarding experience to see that so many of us were still actively involved in the American Indian struggle.

The quality of the newcomers, too, was inspiring. After listening to their thoughts and hopes, and visiting with them later, it was heartening to know that as our hair was turning gray, a new generation had picked up the eagle staff and would carry it into the future.

The ideas expressed during these consultations extended not only to

SMALL CLAY figures.
Makers unknown.
Mexico. 21/8344, 23/2173,
23/3851, 23/5508, 23/8616,
23/8676, 23/8701, 23/9362,
24/795, 24/8392

GALLUP CEREMONIAL, ca. 1940.

Gallup, New Mexico. Lot 179

cultural, museum-related, or even spiritual affairs, but went far beyond. People voiced their anxiety over continuing social injustices, unemployment, lack of adequate medical care, cuts in funds for Indian education, and other debilitating factors imposed on our people by the dominant society. These vital issues go far beyond the mission of the new museum, or its ability to address them. I mention them here because they represent the concerns of Indian people and illustrate the very few forums we have where we can raise them. I believe that the majority of speakers who expressed these things realized that the museum could not realistically solve them, but we had to say them anyway, if only to each other.

In working toward a vision of a museum that related to the American Indian ethos and would be meaningful to Native people, we thought of designing a building that would have an opening above to allow the sun to cast its bright light inside, and creating an opening in the floor to symbolize how some tribes emerged from Mother Earth. To ensure that the museum would be unlike any other, some participants suggested that each visitor should be greeted personally and offered a seat and perhaps a cup of coffee, in the way that Indians welcome guests into our homes. Many participants said that all Indian tribes must be represented somehow in the reception area of the museum on the National Mall, perhaps by including a monument built of stones from each community, perhaps by showing flags from every reservation, similar in style to the United Nations.

At every meeting, someone suggested a concept that was truly brilliant, that changed or crystallized our evolving ideas. One such observation was that to truly represent Native people, the museum and its exhibitions and programs should not be shaped by a solely anthropological or historical framework. Instead, it was suggested that to tell our story we would have to invent a new discipline, one that would involve history, anthropology, and other well-established fields, but would equally draw on resources from our communities, including knowledge rooted in oral traditions and kept by our elders and spiritual leaders.

As the discussion continued, someone voiced the realization that no matter how well we planned and built the Heye Center in New York, the Cultural Resources Center in Maryland, and our museum on the National Mall, these facilities would always be located on the East Coast. More than ninety-five percent of American Indian people live west of Washington, D.C. The proportion is even greater when we include the First Nations of Canada and the indigenous populations of Mexico, Central, and South America. Only a small number of these people will ever be able to visit one of the museum's three sites. So it was suggested that we create a fourth museum (the sacred number four!) whose primary function would be to develop and maintain programs for Native communities that reach the length and breadth of the Americas. The inclusion of this virtual museum related directly to our communities and made the creation of the new museum more meaningful to us all. We also hoped that through outreach we could revolutionize knowledge about our ways for Indian and non-Indian people the world over.

So from the beginning, we have developed programs that bring the museum's resources to people whose paths we might never cross otherwise. The Internship Program invites Native and non-Native students to New York and Washington to learn about working in a museum environment. Native artists who take part in the Native Arts Program can conduct research in museum collections, broaden their contacts in the arts world, and work with their communities. The Visiting

Professional Program offers alternative training experiences to Native professionals who wish to develop skills in museum operations. We have established an Artist-in-Residence Program that gives Native artists the means to work in New York City, or another place of their choosing where they can grow.

We regularly bring Native middle- and high-school students, accom-

SPIRIT OF A NATIVE PLACE

panied by teachers, artists, and scholars, into the museum to work with the collections, usually with objects created by members of their cultural group, and we are developing curriculum materials for schools. We produce extensive radio programming, such as the *Living Voices* series, which features Native profiles, including profiles in Spanish. Exhibitions at both the Heye Center and the museum on the National Mall are developed in conjunction with the communities whose histories and cultures they interpret. Archival photographs and objects from the collections are also made available for display at tribal museums and cultural centers, and books and CDs published by the museum are distributed without charge to tribal colleges and community libraries. Our websites bring the fruits of all these programs to virtual visitors around the world.

Finally, our Community Services Department sponsors workshops in the field on many topics, including collection methods, exhibition development and presentation, repatriation and traditional care of objects, and youth projects on photographic documentation.

People's comments during the museum's consultations in the early 1990s were recorded and distilled by Venturi, Scott Brown and Associates, the architects chosen to put together the museum's master plan. The summary they produced, fittingly entitled *The Way of the People*, continues to guide us on the path we wish to follow. A few of the ideas offered at those consultations are quoted in Duane Blue Spruce's Foreword. Many, many more are reflected in the museum's architecture and exhibitions. I wish we could give credit to the people who contributed them. When meetings were transcribed, however, it proved impossible to identify some speakers. I regret that they, like so many Indian people who appear in old photographs and whose works the museum has collected, have become anonymous.

NUMAKIKI (MANDAN) shirt, mid-19th c. Maker unknown. *Collected at Fort Berthold Indian Reservation, North Dakota. 20/1473*

CHAPTER ONE

As Long as We Keep Dancing

A BRIEF PERSONAL HISTORY

by W. Richard West, Jr.

 can say with complete honesty that I grew up in a log cabin. It stood on the campus of Bacone College, in Muskogee, Oklahoma, a small American Baptist college with a historical mission to educate American Indians, where both my parents taught. The student body of Bacone is still largely Native American, but when I was there, from the late 1940s through the very early '60s, it was about ninety percent Indian, enrolling Native students from all over the United States. At that time, there were no tribally controlled community colleges, and the cabin had served as a sort of transitional residence for students coming off the reservations, many of whom had never lived in houses.

The original cabin consisted of two great rooms, one of which had a fireplace tall enough for me to stand up in until I was six or seven. The other had apparently served as a bedroom. Because there were four of us—my father, for whom I am named, already an accomplished painter and sculptor when I was young; my mother, a wonderful pianist; and my brother Jim,

RICK AND JIM West, with their father, preparing for a dance performance, 1956.

three years younger than I—the college built a kitchen and bedroom onto the original structure, in addition to the bathroom, which had been added a year or two before we moved in. We lived there from the time I was about four years old until I was a junior in high school. I went back once, after I'd been away for several years, and was astonished to see how small that cabin was.

My parents met at Bacone in the late 1930s. My father was born in 1912 on what had been until 1891 the Cheyenne Reservation in western Oklahoma. He was educated, from the age of five or six until he was in his early twenties, at Bureau of Indian Affairs boarding schools in Concho, Oklahoma, and Lawrence, Kansas. Others have written about the misguided policies and the sad experience of students at many Indian boarding schools. A Lakota colleague at the museum once told me that her grandfather camped for months at a time outside the fence of his children's school to be near them. My father was removed from his family's home against his parents' wishes. At school, his hair was cut and he was forbidden to speak Cheyenne. Throughout his childhood, he seldom saw his family. His parents later defied authority and refused to let his younger brothers be taken from them.

THE WEST family home on the campus of Bacone College, in Muskogee, Oklahoma, originally served as a small dormitory for students arriving at the college from reservations.

My mother was born in Chefu, in the Shandong Province of northern China, the daughter of American Baptist missionaries, and didn't live in the United States until she was fourteen. She studied at the University of Redlands, in California, another Baptist school, and was no doubt motivated to join the music faculty at

Bacone in part by her family's sense of mission.

I hope I have not made this sound forbidding—growing up on the campus of a Baptist College with a missionary mother. My childhood was, in fact, a very happy one. My parents showed a great deal of respect and affection for each other and for my brother and me. My mother was disciplined, almost to the point of rigidity at times, and my father loosened her up a bit. And despite my father's marvelous creativity, I believe that she had a great deal to do with his success. She had the better business sense, and she was a refuge for him in important ways.

LAKOTA TOY buffalo, ca. 1917.
Maker unknown.
Standing Rock Reservation,
South Dakota. 6/7936

I cannot remember a time when I didn't know I was Cheyenne. My father was quite dark, and I was curious about the distinction between my parents from my earliest childhood. With sixty years' perspective, I see that, in many ways, I have always lived along the borderlands of their two worlds, Native and non-Native. And my experiences in that sometimes-difficult terrain no doubt color what the creation of this museum means to me.

As teachers, my parents had the summers off, and we would take long driving trips to visit relatives in California. We knew all kinds of people on the Navajo Reservation, and we'd stop in New Mexico and Arizona to see friends. We had a great, great time. Those trips are experiences that have a place in memory way out of proportion to their importance then. I remember one summer when we were in Shamrock, Texas, west of Amarillo, on our way to New Mexico. This was an era before anyone phoned ahead for reservations—people just stopped at a motel along the roadside. I'll never forget the name of this particular establishment, the Palomino Motel. My brother and I sat in the car admiring the swimming pool while Mother and Dad checked in. When they came out, my father was stony silent, and I could tell that my mother was furious.

As they got in the car, she said, "We're not staying here." She started to say something else, but my father kind of quieted her down. What had happened was that the Palomino Motel wouldn't rent us a room, because of my father's color. My brother remembers being far more upset than I do. I recall thinking, "Well, that's their problem. There are other motels in town—with swimming pools—and they'll take us." And in fact we found another place very quickly. I thought even then that this kind of prejudice was idiocy, and I wasn't going to be made to feel bad because of it. My brother was more affected by it. My mother was infuriated by it. My father, I think, was equally angry, but buried it, and that was very typical of him.

During the school year, my father sometimes worked in a studio in the college's Art Department, but he also kept an easel in the living room, near my mother's piano, and my mother often practiced while he worked. My brother and I loved to watch him paint, and although there were times he worked alone, he didn't feel he needed privacy to create. I have never really thought of this before, but it strikes me now that his approach was very Indian—Indian creativity is largely communal in nature. He'd let us squeeze paint onto the palettes, or pick out colors we liked, colors that did not necessarily appear in his finished paintings.

My father never "painted Indian" or tried to appeal to the market for "Indian art." Granted, he had the security of a teaching position, but more important, he believed that art was dynamic and that even the most "traditional" art reflects change. As a child I thought no one beaded better than the Cheyenne—no doubt a part of me still believes it—but when my father ordered the beads for my first moccasins, they came from Czechoslovakia, which, he pointed out, had pretty much been the case since beads had become available in Indian Territory more than a century earlier. He saw his own work as a creative path grounded in his Cheyenne cultural identity. That path had led him from an artistic beginning painting flat, two-dimensional representations reflecting the traditions and motifs of the Great Plains to a period of radical experimentation that resulted in abstract work. Before World War II, Lloyd Kiva New, a towering figure in Native American art, in my own life, and in the conception of this museum, had helped my father land his first teaching job, at the Phoenix Indian School, and my father, in turn, championed the work of other Native artists.

The Cheyenne have a proverb, which many tribes no doubt share: "We will always remember who we are as long as we keep dancing." My father taught my brother and me to dance virtually as soon as Jim learned to walk. In addition to being head of the Art Department, Dad was the faculty advisor for the Indian Club, a performance troupe of sorts on campus, and the members of the Indian Club taught us as well. There were several brothers from a talented Kiowa family well known in Oklahoma who studied at Bacone while we were growing up, so we learned to dance to any number of Kiowa songs.

I think my father saw Bacone as a protected place for my brother and me, and it was. I remember one time when I must have been about six years old, when I went to downtown Muskogee to see the latest shoot-'em-up cowboys-and-Indians movie at the Saturday matinee. Over my lengthy protests that I could go by myself—I was born talking, apparently—one of the elderly Indian dorm-mothers from Bacone came along. Leaving the theater, I

AS HEAD of the Art Department at Bacone from 1947 until 1970, Dick West influenced a generation of Native artists. Ronald Red Elk (Comanche), the student shown here, is now president of the Comanche Nation Language and Cultural Preservation Committee and assistant principal of Anadarko High School. Ronald Red Elk and Dick West, ca. 1960. *Muskogee, Oklahoma. P19663*

commented to her that the Indians in the movie didn't look or act like any Indians I knew. At first, she smiled at my literal-mindedness, but she grew thoughtful as we walked. Finally, she stopped and turned to me and said, "Richie, you must never forget that they have no idea who we are."

In 1989, in enacting the legislation that authorized the creation of the National Museum of the American Indian, then-Representative Ben Nighthorse Campbell, Senator Daniel Inouye, and their colleagues in the United States Congress made an unprecedented commitment to involving Native peoples in the representation and interpretation of our cultures. At least that is how I interpret the provision in the legislation that establishes that more than half of the seats on the museum's governing Board of Trustees are to be held by Native Americans. And it is how I see the Smithsonian's decision to select a Native American as founding director. Before I accepted that honor, and challenge, I asked myself not only how the museum could become a place where Native peoples could say who we are, but also whether the larger culture would be willing to accept such an institution. Clearly, I decided that it would.

In addition to acquiring for the Smithsonian the unparalleled collections of the Museum of the American Indian–Heye Foundation and setting us on the course we have taken, the National Museum of the American Indian Act called for the construction of the three facilities that make up the stone-and-mortar face of the museum. The George Gustav Heye Center, which opened in the historic Alexander Hamilton U.S. Custom House in lower Manhattan in 1994, acknowledges New York's long and meaningful association with Heye's endeavor. For me, the Heye Center also stands as a tribute to Senator Moynihan, a steadfast advocate for the creation of this museum and a loyal champion of New York City. The second building, the Cultural Resources Center, completed in 1998 adjacent to the Smithsonian Museum Support Center in Washington's Maryland suburbs, is described in the legislation as a conservation and storage facility, although it has come to be something much closer to a home for the collections. The third building is, of course, the museum on the last available building site on the National Mall.

Given this ambitious conception, I was not terribly surprised when I arrived at the Smithsonian in the summer of 1990 that the first person to ask for an appointment with me was the director of the Institution's Office of Design and Construction. The point he wished to make was that work toward the design and engineering of the museum's buildings was proceeding at an excellent pace, and that what was required of me was to board the moving train as quickly as possible. I asked the first question that came into my mind: "Do we know what is going to go on inside these spaces?" From my perspective, what we wanted to do at the museum would determine the architecture of our buildings. And I felt very strongly that the decisions shaping the museum's programs should be driven by the ideas and aspirations of Native peoples.

So for two years, from 1991 to 1993, with the firm support of the secretary of the Smithsonian at that time, Robert McCormick Adams, the museum put design and construction on hold while we hosted some two dozen consultations throughout the United States and in Canada. The hundreds of individuals who attended these meetings were predominantly, though not exclusively, Native and represented a great diversity of backgrounds and interests. They included Native and non-Native museum professionals and educators, Native elders, Native community and political leaders, and Native artists from countries throughout the Western Hemisphere. No single component of the museum's history is more important than these consultations. They are absolutely essential to it. They have made every bit of difference to the development of the museum.

Over time, the messages that emerged from the consultations had a remarkable clarity. I cannot say that I was surprised by the ideas we heard, although I think some of the other representatives sitting at the Smithsonian's end of the table may have been. Rather, what we heard confirmed many of the things I felt I knew growing up Indian.

First, while acknowledging our deep past, Native peoples want to be seen as communities and cultures that are very much alive today. Second, we want the opportunity to speak directly to museum visitors through our exhibitions and public programs, and to describe in our own voices and through our own eyes the meanings of the objects in the museum's collections and their importance in Native art, culture, and history. And third, we want the museum to act in direct support of contemporary Native communities.

I doubt there is an Indian living in the United States who does not have a story to tell related to the first of these points. The first time my father took Jim and me to a natural history museum, I remember asking why the Indian displays were there among the mammoths and the dinosaurs. He answered, "I think they must believe we're dead, too." Just recently, I was talking about the museum with the woman sitting next to me on a plane when she asked, "And are you"—here she paused—"a Native American?" When I said that I was, she asked what tribe I was from. "Cheyenne," I said. Her reaction was, "I thought they were all dead!" With all respect to my Cheyenne ancestors who died at Sand

Creek and to the many millions of Native people who suffered the great tragedies of this hemisphere's history, we are very much alive. At the museum we underscore the fact that we are still here in everything we do, but especially in our emphasis on live performances, discussions, symposia, and other public programs that present contemporary Native individuals and groups.

The rightness of the second point, too—the idea of the museum as a forum where Native peoples interpret our cultural inheritance and contemporary lives from our own perspectives and in our own voices—seems self-evident to me. When I was very young, my father took me with him on a visit to the Philbrook Art Center in Tulsa, Oklahoma, which has a very significant collection of Native American objects. I remember a Tlingit carving in particular. My father spoke about the artist's technical skill as a sculptor, the use of color, the composition, design, and line of the piece. Then he smiled and said, "Of course, none of that is what it really means. For the Tlingit, its meaning lies in its spiritual use."

Many years later, at the Millicent Rogers Museum in Taos, New Mexico, I was standing before an exhibit case looking at a ceramic pot sculpted by the hand and spirit of the wonderful San Ildefonso Pueblo artist Popovi Da. The pot was exquisite, and I was content to stand there in silence for a very long time, taking in its beauty. Finally, my eye moved to a brief text that had been placed next to the case, a statement by Popovi Da himself. The words spoke volumes about his world and how his art was related to it:

> *We do what comes from thinking, and sometimes hours and even days are spent to create an aesthetic scroll in design.*
>
> *Our symbols and our representations are all expressed as an endless cadence, and beautifully organized in our art as well as in our dance. . . .*

GRAPHIC INTERPRETATION
of the Sun Dance, late 19th c.
Painted by Black Chicken
(Yanktonai Dakota).
Fort Peck Reservation,
Montana. 2/3304

DICK WEST saw art as a creative path, although his work was always grounded in his Cheyenne identity. This early painting depicts a story from Cheyenne oral tradition and shows the nation before it migrated from the Woodlands to the Plains. Later, West experimented with abstract styles. *Dark Dance of the Little People,* 1948. Painted by W. Richard West, Sr. (Southern Cheyenne).
Muskogee, Oklahoma. 25/8382

AS LONG AS WE KEEP DANCING

There is a design in living things; their shapes, forms, the ability to live, all have meaning. . . . Our values are indwelling and dependent upon time and space unmeasured. This in itself is beauty.

Please note that the National Museum of the American Indian is not the first or only museum to recognize the importance of presenting Native perspectives on Native art. Nor will we exclude the voices of non-Native scholars from the interpretation of Native cultures. We have, however, gone an unprecedented distance down the path of Native representation and interpretation by inviting whole Native communities, from North, Central, and South America, to say what they would like to say in the extensive community-curated sections of our exhibitions.

One last story from my childhood: when I was thirteen, my father took my brother and me on a trip to New York City. It was the first time Jim and I had been east of the Mississippi River—to tell the truth, it was the first time we'd been east of the east side of Muskogee. The trip was a cultural pilgrimage for us, and our goal was the Heye Foundation's Museum of the American Indian, then in its last venue, at Audubon Terrace in upper Manhattan. To my artist father's mind and eye, the Heye collections contained the finest examples of Cheyenne cultural material to be seen anywhere. I remember thinking, as we were shown drawer after drawer of beautiful Cheyenne pipes, pipe bags, clothing, ceremonial regalia, and shields, that I was looking at a significant part of the history of the Cheyenne nation. And I remember asking my father, specifically, whether the Cheyenne people at home in Oklahoma knew what was there and would ever be able to see it. I find myself in a position, many years later, to answer my own question. And the answer is, they will.

Support for Native communities stands at the very center of what the museum seeks to do. This ethic is reflected in our exhibitions, publications, internships, and visiting artist and scholar programs; in our use of media, including the Internet and Native radio (by far the most accessible and far-reaching communications technology on the reservations); and in our commitment to the repatriation of culturally sensitive collections. We refer to our work with Native peoples and communities as the fourth museum, to remind ourselves that how well we reach Native communities is every bit as important to our mission as what we do at the Heye Center, the Cultural Resources Center, and the museum on the National Mall.

Behind all this lies a reality that challenges a precept in some ways still held, I think, by the majority culture in the United States—the idea of our nation as a melting pot. Very little nonfiction has been written about the inner life of lawyers, for very good reasons, I suspect. But I would like to share one experience from the fifteen years of my life when I was, in fact, an attorney practicing Indian law. For more than sixty years, on and off,

the Lakota Nation pursued a claim against the United States government for return of the Paha Sapa, the Black Hills of South Dakota, which were taken by an act of Congress in 1877. They were taken largely because gold deposits had been discovered there, though also in part in retribution for the overwhelming defeat of the U.S. Army at the Battle of Little Big Horn in 1876. Paha Sapa has been translated "the heart of all that is." The hills are the holiest of places for the Lakota, a place of vision quests,

and home to Wakan Tanka, the Great Spirit, the sum of all that is powerful, sacred, and full of mystery.

I did not argue the case for the Lakota when it came before the U.S. Supreme Court in 1980, but I did have the privilege of working extensively on the brief. The court upheld the tribe's claim and awarded the Lakota $106 million, the largest judgment ever entered in favor of an Indian tribe for lands taken by the United States. Yet the Supreme Court's ruling is not the end, or even the most important point, of the story. That judgment, awarded more than two decades ago, still sits on account in the U.S. Treasury and, by my last tally, was worth the better part of a billion dollars. A majority of the Lakota people, despite their very real material poverty, refuse to take the government's money because they feel that such an act would compromise their legislative efforts to regain at least a part of their beloved sacred lands.

Literally every community of the Native Americas can tell a similar story

of cultural persistence. As a Cheyenne, I think of Bear Butte, located in western South Dakota just beyond the Black Hills. According to our teachings, it was there that Mitsuehuevi, perhaps our most important spiritual leader, spoke with our earliest forebears, an event that stands at the beginning of time. Even now, well into the twenty-first century, on almost any given summer day, prayer cloths can be seen tied to the branches of the trees that dot the sides of the butte as Cheyennes make their pilgrimage to this holy place in an act of spiritual renewal.

Many Native peoples see time as a circle. Yet even if we look at time as a linear measure, the period from 1877 to now is a brief moment in the great span of cultural history, and 1492 itself is not so long ago. If the American experience to the present day demonstrates anything, it is that Indian cultures have not melted, even in the face of great heat.

A few years ago, I was in Cheyenne country in Oklahoma, in part to make a report on the museum to the tribe, which we do from time to time. I know many of the older chiefs, and after dinner they invited me into their tipi to sit and talk. They told me that they were considering making me a chief, and wondered how I felt about that possibility.

My memory of that night is very clear. The tipi was not far from the Concho boarding school my father attended. An uncle, a chief of the Cheyenne, is buried in the cemetery nearby, as well. I sat in the tipi, with the wind blowing as it does on the Plains in the spring and the tipi flaps banging back and forth, a sound so familiar to me. And the significance of that moment was not even so much the deeply humbling thought, "It's possible I will become a chief." It was more personal than that. I felt, in a very profound way, "I'm home."

Becoming a chief is a very deliberate process, appropriately so, and a very informal process. There is no search committee. There are no votes. Instead, I was expected to visit with people, many of whom I'd known for a long time, others whom I hadn't known before. I went back to Oklahoma for the Sun Dance that July. The chiefs meet the night before the dancers go in for the Sun Dance. The chiefs' tipi is much bigger than the others, because it has to seat more people, and it always occupies a very particular place on the Sun Dance grounds and faces a particular direction. I had dinner that night with one of my sponsors, and we sat and talked. Then the chiefs went into the tipi. I had been told that people would come out to get me, probably at about eight o'clock. Well,

THREE GENERATIONS of the West family danced at the pow-wow celebrating NMAI's first exhibition, *Pathways of Tradition*, which opened in 1992 in New York. (From left to right) Dick West, Rick West, Jim West, Rick's son, Ben, and Jim's daughters, Karin Weekes and Christina McDonald.

shortly after midnight my sponsors came, and my second sponsor turned out to be an Arapaho man I knew very well from when I was an attorney. Four Arapahos sit among the forty-four Cheyenne chiefs. That has been true for probably 300 years, and it is still true. Being sponsored by someone from beyond my own tribe meant a great deal to me. The two men took me into the big tipi and had me sit in a particular place. And then the conversation went around the room, and everyone gave me advice. They gave me counsel, much of it in Cheyenne.

When they asked me to come into the tipi that night, the chiefs had elected

to have me there, among them. And so the ceremony for me was a matter of listening, and listening well, to their conversation, which went on for a long time. People talked about the fact that it had been a while since someone from our family had been in the Society of Chiefs. I was not there because I was director of the museum, although they said they thought that was wonderful. I was there because of things that are found much closer to home. The most honored place for a chief to sit is directly across from the tipi door, and I was seated near that place. When I wondered if that was appropriate, someone said, "Well, this time we wanted you to sit where your great-uncle, Elliott Flying Coyote, sat." Elliott, who had been one of the four Principal Chiefs, was revered among the Cheyenne.

A chief's role is to support the community, in all kinds of ways. It encompasses helping people. And, of course, it involves supporting the ceremonial life of the community. In the Sun Dance, there is a cry—it's not a Cheyenne cry, it's a Lakota cry—"For the people!" The dancers dance for the people. And the chiefs are there for the people. It is in some ways up to each of us to figure out how that manifests itself and what it means, but the people's welfare, as a community and as individuals, is to be always on our minds.

I have tried to bring that same thought back to Washington. There is a profound connectedness between this museum and Native America. The museum on the National Mall represents the long overdue recognition of the contribution Native peoples and communities have made and continue to make to American civilization. For non-Natives, I believe that the museum will be an invaluable resource for learning about cultures that were here at the very beginning of this country and are woven into its heritage. For the first citizens of this hemisphere, I have faith that the museum will serve as a center of affirmation. Perhaps most important, I believe, the building will become a crucial meeting ground, a place where Natives and non-Natives can achieve the cultural understanding and reconciliation that have eluded us in the past.

I often think of a favorite poem of mine, titled "It Doesn't End, of Course." The writer, Simon Ortiz, of the Pueblo of Acoma, in New Mexico, was writing of his own, personal cultural survival, but his words are a powerful metaphor for all of Native America:

RICK WEST, at home in

Washington, D.C.

> It doesn't end.
> In all growing from all earths to all skies,
> In all touching all things,
> In all soothing the aches of all years,
> It doesn't end.

The museum will be here for a very long time, through the lives of my children, and through the lives of their children. What goes on in it will change over time, as it should, but there will always be this place—this Native place. As long as this country is here, it will be here.

CHAPTER TWO

Carved by Wind and Water

BUILDING A NATIVE PLACE

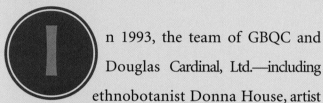

In 1993, the team of GBQC and Douglas Cardinal, Ltd.—including ethnobotanist Donna House, artist Ramona Sakiestewa, and architects Douglas Cardinal and Johnpaul Jones—took up the challenge of designing the museum on the National Mall. The distinctive curvilinear form they created, evoking a rock formation shaped by natural elements, is the basis for the museum's architecture.

Five years later, pleased with the conceptual design but concerned with the progress and coordination of the work, the Smithsonian Institution asked GBQC and Douglas Cardinal to leave the project. The Smithsonian assumed responsibility for finishing the museum with Johnpaul, Donna, and Ramona, along with the architects Jones & Jones, SmithGroup in collaboration with Lou Weller (Caddo), the Native American Design Collaborative, and Polshek Partnership.

Here, the three designers who worked on the building from the first brainstorming sessions through the intricacies of construction describe a creative process that reflects their own experience as Native Americans, as well as the vision of Native cultural and community leaders whose views the museum sought from the beginning.—D.B.S.

ANTELOPE CANYON, LeChee Navajo lands, northern Arizona.

"WE WANT SOME OF US
IN THAT BUILDING"

by Johnpaul Jones

My own involvement with this building began before the National Museum of the American Indian was created. Sometime during the 1980s, I heard that the Heye Foundation was looking for a new home for the collections, and that Ross Perot was interested in acquiring them and moving them to Dallas. I wrote Perot to tell him I would love to work on his project, if it went through.

Clearly—Rick West and others have said this as well—the consultations that began in the early 1990s were essential to the design of this building. The Smithsonian was able to bring Indian elders, Indian artists, Indian educators, and other Indian professionals into the process of creating the museum. One key to the consultations is that the museum staff went to where Indian people live. They didn't simply say, "Come to Washington." That was important to making people feel comfortable with the project, because in the past things have not worked out very positively for Indians in Washington. Meeting with people in their own homelands led to much more open discussions.

One of the consultations in which I took part was held in Vancouver, British Columbia. There were perhaps a hundred people there. One Inuit elder, a woman, said, "You, designers, we're going to be watching you. And we want some of us in that building." We heard that a number of times in different consultations. "We want some of us in that building."

The ideas that arose from those discussions were not limited to architecture, or even to design. Rather, they concerned people's ways of life. How do we deal with each other? How do we deal with the world around us? How do we deal with the animal world, the spirit world? Those are the ideas that

AN ARCHITECT'S model of National Museum of the American Indian captures the building's mass and fluidity.

inspired us when we began to do the initial design. They are not complicated or mystical. They have to do with simple things around us that connect our lives to a world where everything is alive, everything has a spirit.

From the beginning, we offered our services to the museum as a design team: two Indian women—Donna House and Ramona Sakiestewa—and two Indian men—Douglas Cardinal and me. We saw ourselves as a group of people working together to solve a problem. We felt that our different backgrounds and interests would be strengths we could bring to the challenge of designing a museum that hoped to represent all the Native peoples of the Americas. And I think that has been borne out by our experience.

Initially, the site of the museum seemed to have few qualities that we

THE REVISED site plan illustrates key elements of the museum's grounds, including the water feature cascading along the building's north face, and the ceremonial plaza and wetlands to the east.

could relate to, or that other Indian people would relate to. Washington is not a very Native place. It's full of Greeks and Romans; even the trees along the Mall are planted in straight lines. Eventually we learned the area's history and natural history. Before that, however, a group of elders who were serving as advisors on the project walked the site and found its center. I don't know exactly how they identified it, but they buried some things on the site and said, "This is its center." The stone at the heart of the Potomac, the museum's beautiful rotunda, sits at that center point.

We also plotted the cardinal directions and were very conscious not to

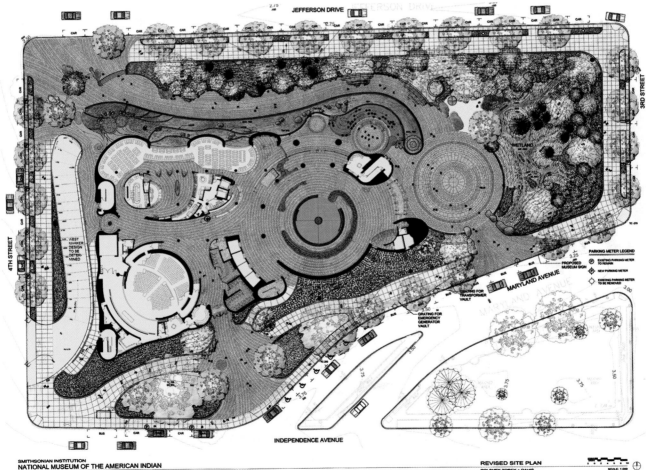

SMITHSONIAN INSTITUTION
NATIONAL MUSEUM OF THE AMERICAN INDIAN
OPP PROJECT No. 922307 DECEMBER 20, 1999

REVISED SITE PLAN
POLSHEK TOBEY + DAVIS
JONES & JONES

obstruct them in the design, so that they flow from the building very easily. I don't mean to overstate this. There are many directions, of course, but those turning points on the earth—where the sun comes up when summer is over and it turns toward fall—were carefully laid out on the site and respected. When Indian elders come to the museum, they will tell stories about how we should conduct our lives, and they will need to know which way is east or west, north or south. All Indian gatherings begin with a prayer. I was at a conference once, in a large building, and the man who was giving the prayer said, "Which way is west? I don't know." So here, that is clear in the architecture.

We also decided that we wanted visitors, most of whom will come from the other museums on the Mall to the west, to walk around our site and enter the building from the east. Not every Indian culture believes that doorways should face east, but it is characteristic of many Indian structures. The east entrance also faces the Capitol, and we placed the wetlands on the east side of the site so that the land would be very open to that view. I think people will be surprised at how close the Capitol appears to be.

People have asked how the architects began the design. Ultimately, we realized that we had done enough talking, we had read enough. It was time to lock ourselves in a room, sit down, and figure out how we were going to take the things we had learned and start pulling them together into what I call a geometry.

Douglas Cardinal's approach to the shape of the building was very straightforward. The project had a height limitation and a setback limitation, to conform to the overall architecture of the Mall, and those limitations left us with a space in which we could build. If we took that three-dimensional space, imagined it as a chunk of rock, and carved into it, as wind and water would do, we could create a design that had a very natural quality to it. Originally, we considered using the same stone that was used for the

THE DESIGN process involved countless consultations and presentations by architects Douglas Cardinal (left) and Johnpaul Jones to ensure that Native people saw their values reflected in the architecture.

exterior of the East Building of the National Gallery of Art, but there wasn't enough of it available. So we chose instead a creamier-colored Kasota stone that is quarried in Minnesota. The museum starts at the base with very large stones with a roughback finish. The main body of the building is faced in split-face stone, which is a little smoother. And then there are highlights—on tight curves, and above and below openings—made of a very smooth, tapestry-finish stone.

Although in some ways the building looks as though it was carved by nature, it shows a human hand as well.

The end of the Smithsonian's relationship with Douglas Cardinal was difficult for me, personally, because he and I are good friends. But I had to make a decision whether or not to stay with the project. I was afraid that if our team was not here and another architect was brought in to finish the building, we risked losing the Indian values that we had put into it. We had put so much into this design, and I didn't want us to turn our backs on the museum. Douglas and I talked about my decision. He said, "Well, you have to do what you have to do, and I have to do what I have to do." We parted ways on a friendly basis. I missed him throughout the project, especially at the end. The architects who were brought on board were very respectful, and we worked together diligently to create this building, which is still very much Douglas's conception. I'm very grateful for that.

The interior spaces are based on circles. The concept of the circle comes up often in Indian thought—in storytelling, for example, and in government. It manifests itself in physical forms as well—tipis are often arranged in a circle, for example. In the Northwest, many traditional carvings and other designs are circular in form.

When I met the contractor who was selected to do the construction, he'd already had a chance to study the drawings. "This is really a simple building," I told him. "It's based on radii and radial points." And he said, "Tell me another story!" When contractors work on a rectilinear building, they look for repetitive elements that will make it economical to build. Here, rather than saying, "Every element of this building is unique," the contractor very creatively analyzed the curves on the surface of the exterior and in other places, then built forms that he could use in more than one place. The bricklayers loved working on this project. Many of them told me it was the most exciting design they'd ever built.

Among the problems we struggled with was how to lay the stone floor when in one area, the circle is based on a certain radius, and in another area, on another radius. We found the solution right in front of us. We were trying to figure out how to make the different radii come together, and I had a couple of bundles of sweetgrass on my desk. Sweetgrass is a fairly common herb used in ceremonies in indigenous cultures, and it's sold in braids. I said, "There it is." I laid a bundle of sweetgrass in front of the other designers, and they saw how we could braid the radii together. There is only one sharp angle in the building, and we fought to eliminate even that. I suspect visitors will take up the challenge of finding it.

It's difficult to explain precisely what makes this a Native place, the elements are so intertwined throughout the whole building. When you step onto the site, it's going to feel different from other places in Washington, more connected to the natural world. The stone pavement of the Welcoming Plaza, outside the entrance to the building, includes a representation of the night sky over Washington on November 28, 1989. It reflects our belief that everything in the world has life. If visitors notice it and ask what it means, the museum staff will tell them that it marks the day the legislation establishing the National Museum of the American Indian was signed. It's a birth date, the day the museum came alive.

LATE AFTERNOON sunlight on the southwest corner of the building highlights variations in the Kasota stone. The use of stone blocks of different sizes contributes to the handmade quality of the building.

THE LAND HAS A MEMORY

by Donna House

DONNA HOUSE makes her home in New Mexico, but her work identifying species and helping to protect their habitats has led her to visit communities throughout the Americas.

I am born into my Diné maternal Kinyaa'nii Clan, Towering House People, and born for my Oneida/Navajo paternal Turtle Clan. My Diné maternal grandfather clan is Tsi'naajíí, Black Streaked-Wood People, and my Diné paternal grandfather clan is Tl'izłani, Many Goats People. For almost two decades, I've worked with Native communities, identifying rare and culturally important plant species and protecting their habitats. When we lose species, we lose our culture and language. The words we use and the stories we tell are a journal of the life history of plants and their pollinators, the stars in relation to plants, and many other complex relationships undiscovered and unrecognized by the scientific method.

For the Diné, or Navajo, people, our relationship with the land begins at birth. The family buries the baby's umbilical cord close to home, in the belief that the child will always return there. I was born in Washington, and although my mother didn't follow the tradition, she reminded me of it when I told her I was going to be a part of this project. Before I started work, I reintroduced myself to the land, hiking its trails and canoeing the Potomac. I embraced my curiosity about the earliest plant specimens collected in the Americas. NMAI Deputy Director Doug Evelyn and Peggy Olwell, of the Native Plant Alliance, introduced me to prominent architects and botanists in Washington. I worked my way through the species, scholarly journals, and rare books at the National Herbarium, a collection almost as old as the Smithsonian itself, curated by the Botany Department of the Natural History Museum; the U.S. Botanic Garden; and the National Arboretum. I researched the Mall site at the National Park Service Center for Urban Ecology.

I also researched the plants used to make many of the objects in the museum's collections. There are duck decoys, for example, made by Native people in western Nevada 2,000 years ago. The Paiute people made similar decoys well into the twentieth century. I wanted to acknowledge them in the landscape. I am happy to say that I identified a species of bulrush found here, as well as in the Paiute regions of Nevada, though I admit I'd still love to pinpoint the specific wetlands where the rushes used to make those decoys grew.

WILD PLACES in the Blue Ridge Mountains and along the Potomac River inspire three of the habitats; the fourth pays homage to the Native croplands of the region.

The original drawings for the museum show a narrow strip of land around the building, but I envisioned habitats where plants and animals would dwell—ecological communities, not simply a decorative landscape. At each design meeting, I'd amend what I thought of as the Strip of Land Treaty to create more space for the habitats. I found a directive calling on the U.S. Park Service to transition to native plants throughout the national parks and used it to further my cause. Now there are 145 different species on the museum's grounds, every one of them native to this region. There are no hybrids or exotic species, no tulips. We planted a total of 27,346 perennials in eight different types of soils.

In laying out spaces on the site for a forest habitat, wetlands habitat, meadow habitat, and croplands, my intention was not to restore the lowland marsh of the eastern end of the Mall, but to re-create a natural area around the museum that would represent the natural places found in this part of the world. The land has a memory. By respecting that memory, we honor the land.

In the end, we worked with eleven nurseries from Connecticut to North Carolina. In the Navajo way, plants are collected with respect and intention, beginning with prayer and with songs to the plant and the specific ecosystem where it grows. Singing the appropriate songs is a way of showing reverence and giving thanks. The response of the nursery staffs to our blessing their seedlings and cuttings has been very rewarding. This will be a perennial landscape, growing or lying dormant with the seasons—far from the plug-in, plug-out approach of so much contemporary landscaping. People are grateful to be a part of it.

The design team and advisors acknowledged an indigenous worldview in which the environment and our dwellings are not separate. There are no lines dividing the museum from the grounds. The habitats are an extension of the exhibitions and architecture. I'll give an example of how that was achieved: I brought a six-centimeter prism to one of the initial brainstorming meetings with Douglas Cardinal and placed it on a focal point of the elliptical conference table. Then I took a deep breath and, before I could lose my courage, exhaled the Diné symbolism and stories that recount how the rainbow protects humanity. Years passed before the design team embraced the idea. Once when Johnpaul and his wife, Marjorie, came to pick nectarines on my farm, I took the opportunity to re-sing my prism chant and

VIRGINIA MAGNOLIA graces the woodlands habitat. All the species planted on the museum's grounds are native to the Piedmont and Coastal Plain.

project two dozen prism bands on the living room wall. During solstices, the prism window in the south wall of the Potomac will cast rainbow bands into the center of the museum.

Many Native groups regard geological formations as the oldest beings on the earth, older than the Five Finger Beings—the human race. During a vision session, Cheyenne elder William Tallbull described boulders as our grandfathers. About forty Grandfather Rocks welcome visitors to the site. One large boulder also reflects the sounds of the waterfall, an idea I borrowed from the acoustics of Maya stone ball courts. The rocks that mark the cardinal directions are gifts from Native communities in the four corners of the Americas. The museum asked the people of each community to choose a rock that had meaning to them. The rock representing north is

DUCK DECOYS, ca. A.D. 200.

Makers unknown.

Found in Lovelock cave,
Humboldt County, Nevada.
15/4512D and 15/4513

four billion years old, one of the oldest things on earth; west is newly formed lava from Hawai'i. I think of these gifts as a necklace around the building.

I spoke about all this to one of the Washington commissions that reviewed the museum's design. It was a roomful of people wearing suits—myself included—and partway through the presentation I thought, "I'm making too much of the rocks." Afterward, one of the commissioners took me aside and shyly showed me the well-worn stone he keeps in his pocket—a touchstone and connection to the earth.

One day, when construction of the building was well under way and I could see how the geology of the earth and the

movement of the wind and streams are awakened and represented in the building's curves, I thanked the members of the construction crew. They were building a house for all Native people. At home, we always extended our prayers to include their families and their work.

I believe visitors will understand the connection between the museum and the land. All life depends on the earth and sky. In the Diné way, we believe that people sing reality into being. That's what we've done: we've sung the building into being. The noise of the construction equipment, the sound of the water and of the birds and dragonflies in the habitats, the conversations of the visitors—all are part of the song that makes the museum come to be. It is what the Diné call *hózhó,* harmony and beauty coming about.

THE YAGAN people of Isla Navarino, Chile—the southern-most Native community in the Americas—donated a rock from their ancestral lands at Bahía Mejillones to be used as the museum's direction marker to the south.

MAKING OUR WORLD UNDERSTANDABLE

by Ramona Sakiestewa

I kept a quotation from *The Way of the People* beside my worktable throughout this project. It summarizes some of the hopes people had for the museum during the early consultations: "The architecture, design, and atmosphere of the spaces in mind must reflect a deep understanding of Native values, sense of place, and cultural symbolism." That's always been the touchstone. As a designer, I can go down a certain path, and it becomes my path, or the design team's path. The thought expressed in that quotation reminded me to step back and remember what Native people hope to see in this building.

I think I knew I'd be an artist early on. As a child, I arranged my room as if it were a museum. I made labels for my handful of treasures, and I changed their arrangement every month to showcase different things. Albuquerque was still a small town then, and you could camp on anyone's ranch. I traveled all over the Southwest. Every summer we'd stay for days on end at Chaco Canyon before it was a full-fledged park, and at Mesa Verde, really beautiful places. Since then, opportunities to teach and study weaving have taken me all over the world. I realize now that this project allowed me to use everything I've studied, and every place I've ever seen.

My initial role on the design team was to establish a visual vocabulary that the architects and exhibition designers could use—a palette of colors, finishes, and icons for the museum's interior. In consultations, when we asked what the museum should look like, people said, "I see Indian colors," and when they described them, what they saw in their mind's eye was different from what the people at the last meeting had seen. Or people would say, "It needs to be Plains colors." But what does that mean—the colors of a nineteenth-century quilled horsemask, or those of a contemporary dance outfit?

TEXTILE ARTIST Ramona Sakiestewa, shown here in her studio at home in Santa Fe, studied objects in the collections to develop color palettes and design motifs for different spaces within the museum.

So Lloyd New suggested that I do a color study of the objects in the Heye collections. I used Color-Aid paper swatches, a popular design tool, and matched colors to different objects, from different cultures and time periods. It quickly became clear that there are indeed tribal colors, some dictated by the environment, some by the materials available to people, and some simply by the community's preference. The glass beads used for beadwork were imported from Czechoslovakia, and virtually the same palette was available to every tribe, but different groups preferred different colors.

Once I thought I had a sense of all this, I tested my observations by asking two of our design advisors, Susie Bevins, who is Inupiat, and Alma Snell, who is Crow, to look through the stack of Color-Aid samples and choose the ones they felt represented their cultures' colors. Without reference to the museum's collections, which I'd been working from, Susie chose a set of paper swatches that corresponded exactly to the colors of a particular Inupiat object, and Alma chose colors I had identified from Crow objects, plus one color I hadn't seen.

At that point, I glued different sets of color samples to sheets of poster board, along with photographs of objects from the collections and images of nature I'd cut from magazines. I took the boards to half a dozen meetings around the United States and asked people whether what they saw felt right to them. It was an opportunity for everyone to say, "That's definitely not my tribe. It's too messy, too busy. It will never work." I did the same thing with materials and textures we were considering. What makes something feel authentic? When people said there should be wood used in the design, did they mean the smooth wood of a Northwest Coast rattle or the rough, painted wood of a Yamana mask?

When they said there should be water, what did they see in their mind's eye? Sound turned out to an important element in experiencing water, which led us toward the cascading stream along the north façade. That's how I began.

I had done similar things for specific groups—I enjoy extracting the cultural essence of a people, based on artifacts, artwork, landscape, architecture. The museum was particularly difficult, though, because we were trying to represent 500 indigenous groups from throughout the Americas. In the end each interior space has a palette of colors and a motif or icon grounded in nature, the animal world, or abstractions of astronomical configurations.

The sun, for example, is the icon for the Potomac. Sun symbols from different cultures are etched in the glass of the museum's main doors. The annual migration of the sun in our sky is worked into the patina of the woven copper screen that leads visitors into the main space. A shaft of sunlight comes through the oculus at the center of the roof dome. And the light refracted by large prisms set in a narrow window in the south wall of the Potomac will trace the path of the sun through the day.

The colors and finishes in the theater are inspired by the cultures of the Northwest Coast, Alaska, and the Arctic. Native theater largely comes out of night ceremonies, so the moon is an icon for that space, as is Raven, the storyteller. The house lights in the ceiling mirror the constellations of the night sky in Washington. We have tried to create a mood of mist and mystery, to evoke the moment when reality is suspended and the audience is caught up in the presentation.

The challenge has been to make all these elements work together, so that different spaces appear related to each other yet are distinctive throughout the building. Many of the solutions arrived out of a creative discussion among the design group. The copper screen wall, for example, was very much a collaborative solution to the problem of creating a break between the Welcome Area and the Potomac. I no longer remember who came up

KUNA MOLA, ca. 1960.

Maker unknown.

San Blás, Panama. 25/5187

USING COPPER, an ancient metal, and timeless basketry weaves, the designers created a contemporary installation piece for the Potomac.

with the idea. Ilze Jones, Johnpaul's partner, did the structural design and worked with the very talented people in the A. Zahner metal shop. We all critiqued the screen's fabrication. The image is of the rim of a very old basket or bowl all but buried in the earth. We chose to use copper in part as a reference to the antiquity of Indian people on this site. Copper was a widely used material in Moundbuilder cultures, which settled the country from the Great Lakes to the Gulf of Mexico east of the Mississippi, and lasted from 500 B.C. to A.D. 400.

My grandfather used to play the clarinet in a Hopi band. He lived in Tuba City, Arizona, then, and he'd drive to Oraibi once a week to practice. The band played in Washington once, and the thing that made the greatest impression on him was how much water there was. He told me, "You know, when I die and I meet my great-grandfather, who was Chief Tuvi, who moved our family from Oraibi to Tuba City, I'm going to ask him why he didn't come to Washington, D.C., where there was water." Water was the big issue to him. It didn't matter that it was on the other side of the country. Our family had the chance, we could have come to Washington just as well, but we wound up in Moencopi instead. There is no place in this hemisphere where Indian people have not walked. That's

SPIRIT OF A NATIVE PLACE

part of the reason I feel so strongly about our having a museum on the National Mall.

I have so many wishes for this place. I hope visitors will get over the notion that we've lived in the same place for thousands of years—although perhaps that's a Hopi thing. Indians interacted, intermarried, split off, and moved across the country. Native America is not a stagnant, neatly compartmentalized group of cultures. I hope people who come to the museum will recognize that central Mexico was a cradle of civilization, just as Mesopotamia and the Mediterranean world were. I hope they'll learn that Indians have always lived by science and technology. Cultures made a study of astronomy—the astronomical symbolism of the Welcoming Plaza is no different from marking a solar event in a medicine wheel, or on a Maya stele. We understood weather patterns and the migration of animals. We had a knowledge base that made the world understandable.

My greatest hope is that Native people who come to the museum will identify with some of the things we've done, and that non-Natives will think, "This feels different from the rest of the Mall." I. M. Pei's design for the East Building of the National Gallery is completely appropriate to the intellectual art that is, for the most part, exhibited there. But the emotional impact of that design comes from the sharp, finite edge of the southwest corner of the building. People go over to touch it, because they can't quite believe that an angle like that can exist in architecture. It won't matter to me whether people who visit the Indian museum actually articulate to themselves, "This feels different," as long as that emotional impact is there.

DESIGNS INSPIRED by Native symbols and artworks are used throughout the museum. Stylized birds decorate the elevators.

CHAPTER THREE

George Gustav Heye

THE MUSEUM OF THE AMERICAN INDIAN

by Mary Jane Lenz

When the U.S. Congress created the National Museum of the American Indian in 1989, the institution had existed for seventy years as the Museum of the American Indian, also known as the Heye Foundation. The museum and its collections arose from the vision of one man, George Gustav Heye (1874–1957), a wealthy New York banker who managed over some sixty years to acquire the largest assemblage of Indian objects ever collected by a single person. Now including more than 800,000 objects, Heye's collections range from old (10,000-year-old Clovis points) to new (baseball caps with tribal logos); from large (a forty-two-foot-tall totem pole) to small (tiny gold beads from ancient Ecuador); from the north (an ivory carving from Point Barrow, Alaska) to the south (a bone spear point from Tierra del Fuego, collected during Charles Darwin's voyage on the *Beagle*). When Heye died, an obituary written by a long-term colleague stated, "His museum is his monument."

Why a rich New Yorker would become so dedicated to collecting Indian objects remains in some ways a mystery. Late in his life, Heye destroyed most of his personal records, so information about

GEORGE HEYE, his hands on a friend's shoulders, surrounded by schoolmates, ca. 1895. *New York City.* N38372

him is difficult to come by. We do know he came of age during the years when great museums were being developed in the United States—the American Museum of Natural History (founded in 1869) in New York, the Field Museum (1893) in Chicago, to name two of the most prominent. In addition, during Heye's lifetime Native people were both denigrated as savages and romanticized as children of nature. Indians were being driven onto reservations and reserves, sent to boarding schools for acculturation and to mission churches for Christianization, and forced to abandon their languages and ceremonies. It was widely believed that the Native peoples of the Americas were dying out, and that it was only a matter of time before they would disappear altogether. Such anthropologists as Franz Boas were making field trips to Indian Country to collect objects and take notes on Indian languages before it was too late. Many museum collections were begun as attempts to preserve what was left.

Within this social and cultural milieu, George Gustav Heye was born on September 16, 1874, into a world of wealth and privilege. His German-born father was an early associate of John D. Rockefeller at Standard Oil; his mother came from an old New York family and was heir to a cattle-trading fortune. Heye had a sheltered and coddled upbringing, attending private schools and traveling regularly to Europe. His mother and his nurse called him "Baby George" until he entered college. Nothing suggests that he was interested in Indians except for a comment he once made about hunting for arrowheads along the shore of Lake Hoptacong during the childhood summers he spent in New Jersey. In 1892, when Heye was eighteen, he entered Columbia College's School of Mines, where he majored in the newly established discipline of electrical engineering. He lived at home, drilled with the Seventh Regiment Armory in his spare time, and seemed destined for a life much like his father's.

Heye did like the outdoors, however, and his favorite part of the engineering profession was the fieldwork. When he was twenty-three years old and working on a bridge-building project in Kingman, Arizona, Heye acquired his first Indian object. He later wrote:

I obtained a number of Navaho Indians for use as laborers for grading the right of way. I lived in a tent on the work and in the evenings used to wander about the Indians' quarters. One night I noticed the wife of one of my Indian foremen biting on what seemed to be a piece of skin. Upon inquiry I found she was chewing the seams of her husband's deerskin shirt in order to kill the lice. I bought the shirt, became interested in aboriginal customs, and acquired other objects as opportunity offered, sending them back from time to time to my home at 11 East 48th Street. In fact, I spent more time collecting Navaho costume pieces and trinkets than I did superintending roadbeds. That shirt was the start of my collection. Naturally when I had a shirt I wanted a rattle and moccasins. And then the collecting bug seized me and I was lost. When I returned to New York after about ten months in Arizona, I found quite an accumulation of articles. These I placed about my room and I began to read rather intensely on the subject of the Indians.

In 1901, two years after his father's death, Heye gave up engineering and went to work on Wall Street, where he and two colleagues founded an

HEYE LABELED every object in his collections by hand, beginning with this pottery bowl. His numbering system remains distinctive. Ancestral Pueblo Grayware bowl. ca. A.D. 1100–1250, maker unknown. *Tularosa Canyon, New Mexico. 00/0001*

investment bank. He continued to indulge his collecting hobby. One of his New York sources was Covert's Indian Store on lower Fifth Avenue, also known as Covert & Harrington, Commercial Ethnologists. The store advertised, "Collections illustrating American Indian Life for schools and colleges. Museums supplied with authentic material." A number of early pieces in the NMAI collections are attributed to F. M. Covert. The "Harrington" in the firm was Mark R. Harrington, a young graduate of Columbia University. In time he would become one of Heye's most indefatigable collectors, conducting archaeological digs and visiting more tribes and collecting more objects over a twenty-year period than any other member of Heye's staff. Heye developed other collecting relationships as well. An early friendship with Joseph Keppler, the political cartoonist whose family owned *Puck* magazine, sparked his interest in the Iroquois Indians. As early as 1899, Heye and Keppler traveled to upstate New York on the first of a number of visits. Their friendship, which endured all their lives, was marked in conversation and correspondence by the use of nicknames—"O'owah" (Seneca for screech owl) for Heye, "Gyantwaka," "Wolf," or "Kep" for Keppler.

Heye also made friends with George Pepper of the American Museum of Natural History, and with Marshall Saville, professor of American Archaeology at Columbia, who taught him about scientific recording and systematic collecting. He read about Indians with the same energy he devoted to his collecting. A letter written by Pepper in 1904 to F. W. Putnam at the Peabody Museum introduces "Mr. Heye," who "has become greatly interested in anthropological work . . . is a very wealthy young man and seems to be thoroughly enthusiastic. He has bought all of the anthropological papers of the American Museum . . . and will probably want the greater part of those published by the Peabody." (Then thirty-one, Pepper was a year older than the "wealthy young man.")

In 1903 George Pepper moved Heye beyond the acquisition of individual objects by arranging his first purchase of an entire collection, some 600 pieces of archaeological pottery from New Mexico assembled by Henry Hales. The following year, Heye added another archaeological collection, this time from Arizona. He also bought a number of ethnographic objects in 1904 from the Los Angeles dealer B. A. Whalen, many of them from the Northwest Coast. Two years later, Heye acquired a major Southeastern archaeology collection (including skeletal material) from the widow of a Dr. Joseph Jones of New Orleans.

These seem to have been the watershed years, when Heye transformed himself from a hobbyist to his own version of a professional museum man. He began numbering and cataloguing each object he acquired, starting with a Tularosa bowl from the Hales collection. Heye's numbering system was unique, based on increments of 10,000, and museum staff developed a guide for deciphering it for researchers. Beginning with the shirt in 1897, Heye continued to collect and was indeed still acquiring objects in 1957, the year he died. Until those final years, when his eyesight began to fail, he personally catalogued and numbered each piece in his collections. The old handwritten catalogue cards still bear his careful copperplate script, the numbers on the last objects written large and with a less steady hand. Museum lore holds that his memory for the collections was unsurpassed, that he could pick

up an object acquired years before and recount how and where it was collected and what he paid for it.

In 1904 Heye married Blanche Agnes Williams, and his new wife did her best to set up housekeeping in a spacious apartment at 677 Madison Avenue that was already on the verge of being overrun by his collections. Heye also rented, successively, separate floors in the Knabe Piano building and two floors in a loft building at 10 East 33rd Street. For several years the 33rd Street building was designated as the Heye Museum. The name even appeared on Heye's letterhead. In 1908 Heye loaned a large portion of his collections to the University Museum in Philadelphia, where George Gordon, the director, made him a vice president and head of the American Section. Three large exhibit halls were devoted to "the Heye collection," and Heye paid half the salaries of George Pepper, lured from the American Museum of Natural History, and Mark Harrington, who had abandoned the curio store for a career in anthropology. Heye also supported graduate students who, in exchange for funding for their own field-work, collected objects for the museum, to be shared by Heye and George Gordon. Gordon had every expectation that the arrangement would become permanent and added prize pieces to Heye's collections, among them a Plains shield collected by the artist George Catlin, and Haida and Kwakiutl material collected by Stewart Culin and F. W. Newcombe.

From the beginning, Heye's interests encompassed the Western

Hemisphere, and although his primary focus was always on archaeology, his collections included both archaeological and ethnographic material. He began early on to sponsor archaeological expeditions, many in previously unexplored territory throughout Latin America. In 1904 he supported George Pepper's work in Michoacán, Mexico, and Frank Utley's work in Puerto Rico. In 1906, with funds provided by his mother, Heye sent Marshall Saville to Manabi, Ecuador, an archaeological venture that not only yielded a spectacular collection, but also resulted in a massive two-volume report that remains an important publication. From 1907 on,

REPAIRING POTTERY, 1910.
(From left to right) Fred Mifsud, Edwin P. Coffin, and William C. Orchard.
10 East 33rd Street,
New York City. N35883

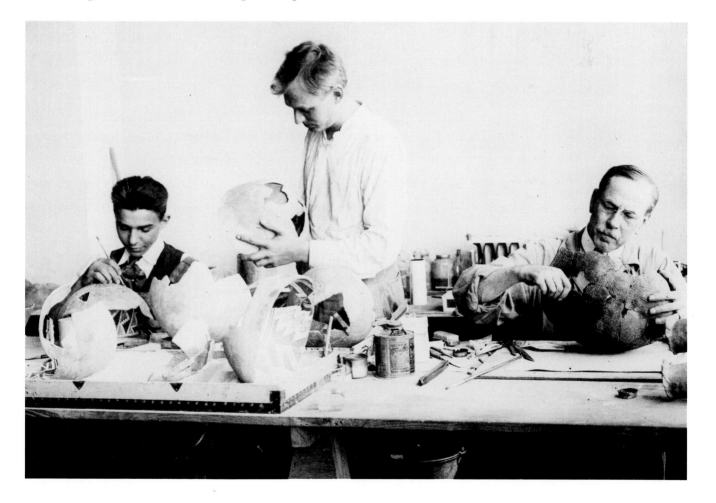

Heye sponsored further archaeological work in the Caribbean, sending Theodore de Booy to the Bahamas, Jamaica, and Cuba, and adding to the collections a huge number of unique objects.

Heye also continued his own collecting, making yearly trips west to acquire objects. Some of the stories about his energy and zeal read like the stuff of legend (and in all likelihood have been embellished)—tales of Heye going into

a Native village and buying everything, down to the shirts on people's backs and the last dirty dishrag, leaving behind only fistfuls of dollar bills; tales of his hiring a car and driver to scour the countryside and, in his impatience, taking over the wheel and speeding down the road at eighty miles per hour while the hapless chauffeur cowered in the back seat. He collected wholesale: rather than carefully choosing one or two of the finest items in an assemblage, he would scoop up the entire lot and take it home. This kind of collecting had its drawbacks: it created storage problems; he acquired many objects that would not have impressed a connoisseur; when he bought from other collectors, documentation of the pieces could be lost. Nevertheless, it was precisely the right method for assembling great research collections.

Consider, for example, moccasins, of which there are approximately 5,000 in the collections. Many of them are exquisitely made and of high aesthetic quality, but many others are dirty and worn out, some with holes in the bottom. This range of condition can help a researcher, a hundred or a thousand years after the object was created, to understand which moccasins were worn every day, and which were saved for special times.

By 1912 his wife had had enough of Heye and his collections and, despite their having two children, she locked him out of their apartment and sued for divorce. (She asked for alimony of $78,000 a year and was awarded $15,000.) The divorce seems to have freed Heye to devote himself to his first love, and he quickly resigned all his Wall Street connections and put his fortune into public-utility stocks. He turned full-time to collecting, excavating, and hiring staff to help build his collections. On his mother's death three years later, Heye inherited a trust worth more than $10 million (a sum conservatively estimated to be worth $150 million today).

Heye's second wife, Thea Kowne Page Heye, like his mother, was sympathetic to his pursuits, so much so that she was willing to spend their honeymoon in 1915 excavating the Nacoochee Mound in Georgia. This major expedition was

HEYE'S SECOND marriage, to Thea Kowne Page, appears to have been far more successful than his first. Thea Heye shared her husband's love of fieldwork and supported his passion for collecting. (From left to right) George Heye, Thea Heye, Harmon Hendricks, and Joseph Keppler, 1919.
Hawikku, New Mexico. N10984

cosponsored with the Smithsonian's Bureau of American Ethnology and managed by the B.A.E.'s chief curator, Frederick Webb Hodge. Hodge, a distinguished scholar, was to bring great prestige to the Heye Museum when he became assistant director. He is also credited with creating a strong publications program there. Heye had by this time also met Charles Turbyfill, a North Carolina farm boy who worked for him for the rest of his life as staff assistant and resident manager of the Research Branch.

There were years when Heye sent as many as six groups out collecting at the same time, sometimes to excavate and sometimes to work with Native people in communities from Alaska to Chile. He also continued collecting with vigor, buying not only individual objects but also entire large collections, such as the assemblage of Capt. D. F. Tozier, a Revenue Service officer who traveled into remote Northwest Coast villages in the 1880s and gathered up house posts and other carvings via questionable methods.

As boxes, barrels, and shipping crates poured into the University Museum from places near and far, it became clear that the collections were going to require a space more substantial than three galleries. They needed a home of their own. At the same time, the noted scholar and philanthropist Archer Huntington, son of railroad tycoon Collis Huntington, dreamed of creating a cultural center for the study of the humanities at Audubon Terrace in upper Manhattan, the site of the old John James Audubon farm.

Huntington had brought together his own Hispanic Society, the American Numismatic Society, the American Geographical Society, and the Academy of Arts and Letters, and he offered Heye a building site and a financial endowment to join this group. Heye accepted. In 1916, the Museum of the American Indian, Heye Foundation, was created. A nearby house on St. Nicholas Avenue was designated as the Physical Anthropology Department (a repository for skeletal material). To George Gordon's consternation, Heye pulled his collections and staff, including George Pepper and

THE 1920s were particularly productive years in Heye's life. He opened the museum at Audubon Terrace in Manhattan, built the Research Branch in the Bronx, and blanketed the Americas with scholars and collectors. Tzutujil Maya filling water jars, 1928.

Lake Atitlán, Guatemala. N14113

Mark Harrington, out of Philadelphia and headed to New York for good.

The opening of the museum at Audubon Terrace was delayed by the onset of World War I, during which the American Geographical Society used Heye's building to house a cartography center for the Navy. Finally, on November 15, 1922, the museum opened. More than two thousand people attended the public ceremony. Heye hosted a celebratory dinner for the Board of Trustees at the Lotos Club, during which they toasted "the time when [the Museum of the American Indian–Heye Foundation] could take its place formally as the leading institution in this country devoted to the scientific study of American Indian archaeology and ethnology."

The neoclassical building, designed by Charles P. Huntington, was adorned with the names of Indian tribes carved into a horizontal band around the building. By 1927 Archer Huntington added to the "Indian" theme by commissioning a pair of magnificent bronze doors, created by the Swiss sculptor Berthold Nebel and decorated with motifs of his own imagining. As he later wrote to Heye, "The complete design of these doors is my own conception of the American Indian. I have tried . . . to illustrate some of their customs and habits as we commonly understand them . . . [in a] series of eight panels (the council; travel; buffalo hunt; women of the prairie; home life; Indian fishermen; religion, the latter showing 'men wearing grotesque masks dancing around a fire'; and returning from the hunt). The ornaments represent symbols—weaving; rattlesnakes; alligator teeth; lynx, serpent and other masks; mountains. All . . . are rough and crude in treatment so as to look brutal in character and supposed to resemble the Mayan or Aztec sculptors in effect and for variety."

The new museum had barely opened when it became clear that the collections were already overflowing the building. The ever-obliging Archer Huntington presented Heye with a six-acre tract in the Pelham Bay area of the Bronx, which became the location of the Research Branch or, as it was

MUSCULAR SCENES of Indian life, as imagined by the Swiss sculptor Berthold Nebel, added to the "Indian" character of Heye's building at Audubon Terrace. Nebel wrote that his border motifs were inspired by "the Mayan or Aztec sculptors." Bronze doors of the Museum of the American Indian–Heye Foundation.
New York City. N20264

informally called, the Bronx Annex. Huntington capped off his gifts to Heye in 1930 when he paid for a modern addition to the Huntington Free Library in nearby Westchester Square as a repository for the Heye Foundation library.

Finished in 1926, the Research Branch was state-of-the-art—a fireproof brick building three-stories tall with seven interior vaults to store the ethnographic collections on the second floor and metal shelving for archaeology on the third. The physical anthropology laboratory moved from the build-

MRS. ALVIN MOFSIE (Seneca), in front of the Seneca cabin on the grounds of the Research Branch, 1943.

New York City. P16102

SPIRIT OF A NATIVE PLACE

ing at St. Nicholas Avenue to a room on the ground floor. It appears that from its inception the Research Branch was intended to serve a public function rather than simply to accommodate a private hobby. The building plan included study rooms where visiting scholars could do research, and the objects were referenced as the "study collections." Moreover, the original plan refers to one room as a "public lecture hall," although there is no record of lectures ever being held there. The architectural features of the Research Branch and the layout of

THE INDIGENOUS garden at the Research Branch. *New York City. N11184*

the grounds further reflected its public intent. The concrete surround of the front door displayed Indian artifacts, including moccasins and masks, while a pair of massive wooden Kwakiutl house posts from the Tozier collection flanked the door frame. An iron fence with finials that resembled stone arrow points was installed in 1927; Archer Huntington paid for that, as well.

Thea Heye worked with staff ethnobotanist Melvin Gilmore to create a garden of indigenous plants, including several types of corn from the Pawnee, Arikara, Omaha, and Winnebago tribes; squash, beans, gourds, and sunflowers from the Arikara and Seneca; three species of tobacco; and cotton, tomatoes, sweet potatoes, red peppers, potatoes, peanuts, and amaranth from Mexico. Columbia University offered its greenhouse for nurturing southern plants, which were then transplanted. Under Gilmore, the students at the local Public School 71 were given garden plots to tend, a

SPIRIT OF A NATIVE PLACE

program copied by the Brooklyn Botanic Garden, as well as by other New York schools.

Over time the grounds of the Research Branch were enhanced by three concrete tipis, a Seneca longhouse, a Pawnee earth lodge, and a Tlingit wooden longhouse and totem pole acquired during the 1899 Harriman Expedition to Alaska. Eventually three other poles joined that one, giving a distinctly exotic appearance to an Irish–Italian neighborhood of the East Bronx and earning the local designation "the Indian reservation." The building and gardens were open to visitors at specified times. As recently as the 1970s, elderly people in the neighborhood recalled that as children they would enter the building and come to a large room with "Indian things" laid out on tables, or that they were allowed to plant things in the garden.

There was also an outreach program in the local schools. In a 1949 letter to Keppler, Heye writes that trustee John Williams had had the "brilliant thought" of celebrating his parents' golden wedding anniversary by sending donations to the museum to continue the school program. During that year, the Heye Foundation loaned the Board of Education two exhibits, which were viewed by 20,000 students and 5,000 adults.

The first years of the new museum were glorious for Heye and those he brought on board to collect for him. Supported by a loyal, affluent Board of Trustees, promised complete freedom to do nothing but research and publish, many of the best and brightest in archaeology and anthropology joined Pepper, Harrington, and William C. Orchard on the museum staff. Alanson Skinner, Samuel K. Lothrop, Donald Cadzow, Theodore de Booy, Thomas Huckerby, Marshall and Foster Saville, Edwin Coffin, and others scattered to bring back both objects and information. Heye's funds also supported the collecting efforts of others, among them scholars such as Samuel A. Barrett, Edward H. Davis, T. T. Waterman, Frank G. Speck, and William Wildschut.

HOUSE POSTS and lintel from the Tozier Collection, flanking the doors of the Research Branch. *New York City. N11089*

The results of this work were published in several monograph series under the aegis of Frederick Webb Hodge. His ambitious publications program brought the museum and its activities to the attention of the scholarly world. Between 1919 and 1921 alone, the annual reports list thirty-seven books and pamphlets published or prepared for publishing, totaling 2,842 pages.

The museum continued to support expeditions throughout the Americas. An excavation at Lovelock Cave, Nevada, yielded a cache of 2,000-year-old reed-and-feather duck decoys, the earliest known in the Western Hemisphere. Between 1916 and 1923, the great Hendricks–Hodge expedition took place to the Zuni village of Hawikku, New Mexico, a site Coronado visited in 1540. Heye paid for expeditions to a rock shelter in Arkansas and an Algonquian site in Vermont, a foray into East Greenland, and a series of expeditions to Argentina, Chile, and Tierra del Fuego, all of which yielded riches for the collections.

In one year, 1924, Heye sent Harrington to Lovelock Cave; Melvin Gilmore to the Omaha Reservation in Nebraska and to the Pawnee and Arikara communities in Oklahoma and North Dakota; S. K. Lothrop to El Salvador and Patagonia; A. Hyatt Verrill to Panama, Chile, Bolivia, and Peru; William Wildschut to the Shoshone and Bannock people in Idaho, the Crow and Cheyenne reservations in Montana, and then to the Blackfeet, Blood, and Piegan communities; E. H. Davis to Mexico; Frank G. Speck to Labrador; and Marshall Saville to Peru. Through expeditions, gifts, and purchases, the collections acquired that year comprised 22,272 objects and 288 photographs, from New Mexico, Argentina, Brazil, Chile, California, British Columbia, Alaska, Guatemala, and upstate New York. The annual report lists 118 individuals or organizations as donors of objects, photographs, books, and paintings. Each of the annual reports for the first decade of the museum's existence documents similar activities, and reflects a thriving operation.

It has often been stated that Heye cared little about the documentation of

HEYE DID not record how this box was used. It may have been a hunter's tally or, despite his admonition against "tourist material," it may have been made for sale. The ivory carvings appear to represent different types of birds. Eskimo box and cover, ca. 1905. Maker unknown.

Yukon River, Alaska. 16/2008

an object, that he was wont to throw away field notes, and that in at least one case he discarded seventy barrels of potsherds for which he had no use. Evidence does suggest, however, that when he engaged others to carry out field collecting, he issued them precise instructions. The NMAI archives include an *aide memoire* written by Donald Cadzow at the time he was hired to forage among the Blackfoot and Cree in Canada. Cadzow carefully copied out Mr. Heye's "My Golden Rule":

> *Every object collected add field tag.*
> *Material must be old.*
> *Hunting outfits*
> *fishing outfits*
> *costumes*
> *masks and ceremonial objects, also dance objects*
> *household utensils particularly stone*
> *and pottery dishes and lamps*
> *Talismans, hunting charms,*
> *all ivory carvings (old)*
> *NO TOURIST MATERIAL*

Heye seems to have made a real effort to preserve information on the objects he collected himself. Letters in the NMAI archives ask donors for additional information on acquisitions. Correspondence with Julius Carlebach, a Madison Avenue dealer with whom Heye had a long

relationship, refers several times to the need for documentation. A May 14, 1953, letter states:

Right now I have quite a few specimens waiting to hear from you further as regards their provenance and I can well understand that the place of origin is not as important to lovers of art as it is to archeological and ethnological collectors. The point of view for purchasing an ethnological piece is entirely different from the artistic point of view than it is from the scientific one.

As you know, I have quite a few pieces that we would love to have but they are not of any value to us unless we can find out where they were found; so, I am beginning to get quite impatient about either returning them to you or keeping them in the hope that you can find out, from the lists you already have, the location of the pieces. . . .

INUPIAT ESKIMO carving, ca. 1900. Maker unknown. Point Barrow, Alaska. 5/4317

Heye traveled yearly to London and Paris, where he picked up wonderful early material that had been carried to Europe during the fur trade. He also swapped with other museums, a common practice at the time. From the U.S. National Museum (now the Smithsonian National Museum of Natural History), he acquired Alaskan objects originally collected by E. W. Nelson around 1880, as well as a Clatsop skirt first acquired by George Catlin. The Field Museum in Chicago yielded early Hopi katsina dolls collected by a missionary. Heye exchanged objects with his old friend and fellow collector Rudolf Haffenreffer in Rhode Island and with George Gordon at the University Museum in Philadelphia.

And Heye purchased from many dealers, although they are not identified as such on the catalogue cards; Stadhagen in Victoria,

Belle Simpson's Nugget Shop in Juneau, Grace Nicholson in Pasadena, W. Oldman in London, and Charles Ratton in Paris are identified by name only. Heye had a long-standing relationship with J. D. Standley's Ye Olde Curiosity Shop in Seattle, which is still in business. From Standley, he acquired dozens of tiny Eskimo ivory carvings, a mammoth tusk, ivory cribbage boards, and Northwest Coast feast spoons. But the Standley pieces are always identified on the catalogue cards as from the "J. D. Standley collection," not from "Ye Olde Curiosity Shop." Kate Duncan, in a recent book on Standley, suggests that it's quite likely that more museum collections have been acquired from curio shops than has generally been recognized. By acting as middlemen for museums that could not afford far-flung expeditions, curio shops often helped build collections. For Heye, they undoubtedly provided opportunities to fill in empty spaces.

Heye could be profligate when he chose and penurious when that suited him. In 1922 he paid what was considered at the time an astronomical sum ($435) for thirty-five of the most striking masks and regalia from the Cranmer potlatch collection. This was an assemblage of more than 400 ceremonial masks, headdresses, and other regalia confiscated by the Royal Canadian Mounted Police from some Kwakiutl people who were celebrating a potlatch at Village Island near Vancouver. The Canadian government, dismayed by what it regarded as an unchristian waste of time and money, had declared the potlatch, a traditional gift-giving ceremony, illegal. The Mounties had seized the regalia, transported it to the nearby town of Alert Bay, and there handed it over to the local Indian agent, William Halliday. Heye appeared on the scene while the pieces were on display at the local church hall. The MAI annual report for that year described the transaction thus: "As the Indians felt they would not have further use for this class of material, a large amount of it was obtained for the Museum, including

NMAI CONTINUES to add contemporary works to the collections. Gourd basket made of cast bronze and coiled bear grass, 2003. Made by Terrol Johnson (Tohono O'Odham). *Sells, Arizona. 26/2578*

several very unique mechanical masks, many head-dresses, rattles, besides utilitarian specimens." Three years later, on another visit to Alert Bay, Heye picked up eleven more Kwakiutl pieces, this time purchased from a B. E. Angermann (probably Bertha Angermann, wife of Sgt. Angermann, the Canadian mounted policeman who had assisted Halliday in the original confiscation). These pieces are identified on the catalogue cards as the "B. E. Angermann collection," and several of them appear in photographs taken at the time of the original confiscation. In the 1990s, when the families of the people who had attended the Cranmer potlatch began repatriation efforts, museum staff did considerable detective work to sort out the Cranmer pieces from the other material from Cape Mudge and Alert Bay that Heye had purchased during the same trip.

In 1928 the museum suffered financial disaster when two of its most devoted board members, James B. Ford and Harmon Hendricks, died within a few days of each other. Each left a bequest to the museum, but the steady flow of income on which Heye had depended had dried up. Heye's immediate response was to fire his entire curatorial staff except for Turbyfill and to end all scientific work. Heye also fired some security guards and cut back on the hours the museum was open to the public. Up until this time, it had been open daily and year-round; Sunday attendance averaged around 1,500 visitors.

Curatorial research was forgotten throughout the 1930s, but collecting was not, and the Great Depression only increased opportunities to acquire collections. Perhaps Heye's single biggest coup was acquiring the incomparable C. B. Moore collection, sneaking it undetected away from the Academy of Natural Sciences in Philadelphia, where it had been one of the treasures of the institution. Clarence Bloomfield Moore was a wealthy "gentleman archaeologist" who, between 1891 and 1918, had carried out major excavations in the Southeast, acquiring superb ceramic vessels, stone pipes,

BEAR MASK, 1990.
Made by Rick Bartow (Mad River Band of Yurok).
Oregon. 25/4798

and other antiquities from the ancient mounds along the rivers. He published at his own expense nineteen lavishly illustrated field reports, providing important documentation for his finds.

Moore and Heye had known each other for years. Moore was an early MAI trustee and a frequent donor of objects, but he had resigned from the board for health reasons in 1924 and was living in Florida. The bulk of his magnificent collection, some 35,000 pieces, remained at the academy in Philadelphia, watched over by Harriet Newall Wardle, the curator for archaeology. In 1929 the academy's president, a banker, decided to dedicate the academy's operations to natural science and to put everything else into storage. When Heye learned of this impending change, he set his sights on the Moore collection, offered cash on the barrelhead and secrecy from the press, and gained Moore's support to move the collection to New York by writing him, "I will do anything in the world to help along the transaction as I know positively this is the place for your magnificent collection, where it will be taken care of properly, will be of use to science, will not be neglected and will be personally loved." When Heye's representatives arrived to unlock the cases and begin removing the collection, Wardle protested vigorously. One account describes the conflict as a comedy of butterfly versus sumo wrestler—Wardle was a tiny woman. She resigned on the spot, later writing an article for *Science* magazine describing the "wreck of the Archaeological Department of the Academy of the Natural Sciences of Philadelphia." But Heye got his way, and considered it his greatest personal achievement. Years later, after both Heye and Wardle were gone, Heye's successor reminisced, "This little lady is now dead, but even when she was well into her nineties she never met a member of the Heye Foundation, or heard its name mentioned, without a glitter in her eye and a tightening of her lips."

Some of Heye's collecting tactics even then seemed buccaneer in their ruthlessness. Assistant Director E. K. Burnett described a visit to the home of

THE MUSEUM of the American Indian did little to encourage visitors between 1929 and Heye's death. Even so, the exhibits at Audubon Terrace remain a fixture in many New Yorkers' memories. Museum of the American Indian–Heye Foundation, ca. 1930.
New York. N20865

Maj. J. A. L. Moller, a wealthy collector of Indian objects and Mexican antiquities who lived in nearby Westchester County, New York. Heye and William Stiles, curator at the Research Branch, were invited to Moller's house one evening to see his collection, which included several pieces displayed on the living room walls. According to Burnett, while the Major was mixing drinks

INKA GOLD figure of a woman, ca. 1500. Maker unknown.

Peru 5/4120

in the kitchen, Heye pointed to the wall decorations and said to Stiles, "Take those down and put them in the car." When Moller returned, Burnett wrote, "If he missed anything on the walls, he didn't say anything about it and he certainly remained a very good friend of the Museum until his death." But Burnett added, "Dr. Heye and I drove out to Moller's several times for luncheon and, if he had made any further collections of Indian material, he certainly kept them off the walls."

At least once in his long collecting career, Heye gave something back. In 1907 in North Dakota, a Presbyterian missionary who had been collecting for Heye purchased from a Hidatsa man a sacred shrine containing a medicine bundle with two skulls and various accoutrements, a bundle that had the power to bring rain. In the 1930s drought struck the Great Plains, and after long negotiations between the Hidatsa leaders of the Water Buster clan and the museum (John Collier, commissioner of Indian affairs, came down on the side of the Hidatsa), Heye finally agreed to return the bundle, "solely for the purpose of cementing the cordial relationship which has always existed between the Museum and the various Indian tribes." In 1938, with the press covering the event, Drags Wolf, seventy-nine years of age, and Foolish Bear, eighty-four, appeared in full regalia at Audubon Terrace, presented Heye with a sacred powder horn and war club, and received in exchange the Water Buster bundle. To their dismay, Heye handed it over one piece at a time. This represented a serious breach of Hidatsa beliefs, for only bundle guardians were supposed to touch the contents. According to one account, the problem was resolved by bestowing on Heye the name "Isatsigibis" or "Slim-Shin," the name of a previous guardian. Drags Wolf and Foolish Bear took the bundle home, and the following spring the rains returned to North Dakota.

It was not until four decades later, when the museum was undergoing the first complete inventory of its collections since its founding, that museum staff found hidden away in a stairwell a large wooden box filled with what turned out to be objects that seemed to belong to the Water Buster bundle. Heye had evidently held back a few pieces he could not bear to let go, and had substituted for them contents that might be appropriate for medicine bundles. Because no one had seen the original bundle for several generations, the substitution had not been detected. So in 1977, the rest of the return was accomplished by a museum staff member who traveled to North Dakota for a second repatriation ceremony.

By that time Heye had been dead for twenty years. He will probably always remain something of a mystery—a man of enormous appetites and great contradictions, described by some as generous and kind, by others as cruel; who took careful notes on his neatly numbered objects, yet discarded the field notes of others; who loved his collections, his wife Thea, and his friends, but who was estranged from his children. One or two influential and widely circulated articles, notably

THEA HEYE, Waihusewa (Governor of Zuni Pueblo), Lorenzo Chavez (Zuni), and George Heye, 1923. *New York. N08130*

a 1960 *New Yorker* profile entitled "Slim-Shin's Monument," portray his collecting as a simple wish to own "the biggest collection of Indian things anywhere." According to Junius Bird, "What he wanted them for he never said." But here and there in Heye's correspondence and in the old museum records, we can find hints about what collecting meant to him. Certainly, acquiring a particular treasure seemed to bring out in him a kind of child-

SPIRIT OF A NATIVE PLACE

like joy. In 1947 Heye wrote to his old friend Joseph Keppler, "I cannot tell you how delighted I am that the matter of the collection between you and the Museum is settled. . . . [N]ext to yourself I love and appreciate your collection more than any one. . . . Again, referring to the deal, 'me happy boy!'" A year later, he wrote to Keppler again, "As regards specimens, you are wrong. They are not alone objects to me, but sources of vistas and dreams of their makers and owners. Whether utilitarian or ceremonial, I try to feel why and how the owner felt regarding them."

Heye's accomplishment was prodigious. His single-minded devotion helped preserve objects that have provided inspiration and cultural renewal for Native people from communities throughout the hemisphere. The relationship between museums and Native people has always been a two-edged sword, fraught with the ambiguities of collecting, preserving, and displaying. During the development of *All Roads Are Good*, one of the inaugural exhibitions at the George Gustav Heye Center in New York, Susan Billie, a young Pomo artist from California who visited the Research Branch to select objects for display, neatly summed up those ambiguities: "The first day I was here I felt angry that there are so many Pomo baskets so far away from home. But by the last day I began to feel grateful that there were so many Pomo baskets here, because they were preserved and now I can see them."

Native communities are now developing their own museums and cultural centers, where they will continue to preserve stories and objects they have never forgotten. NMAI is helping by making its collections available for study and display, and by enabling communities to create their own exhibitions, both on the National Mall and back home. George Heye would no doubt be surprised that the "vanishing people" whose artifacts he sought to save from oblivion are alive and well. He would also no doubt be enormously pleased that his life's work has turned out to be such a precious legacy.

CEREMONY TO return a medicine bundle from the collections to leaders of the Water Buster clan. (Foreground from left to right) W. J. Zimmerman, Indian Bureau, Foolish Bear (Hidatsa), Drags Wolf (Hidatsa), George Gustav Heye, 1938. Nearly forty years after the event, museum staff realized that Heye had held onto some of the bundle's contents. In 1977, the museum repatriated the remaining objects. *New York City. N21512.*

CHAPTER FOUR

A Home for the Collections

THE CULTURAL RESOURCES CENTER

by Liz Hill

othing quite like it has ever been done before. Over a four-and-a-half-year period—between spring 1999 and fall 2003—a team of conservators, collections management specialists, and other staff from the National Museum of the American Indian moved 800,000 objects of Native American material cultural patrimony from the museum's Research Branch storage warehouse in the Bronx to its new Cultural Resources Center in Suitland, Maryland. Week after week, month after month, year after year, semitrailer trucks left New York in the early morning hours, making the slow and careful journey south through some of the East Coast's worst traffic, to reach their destination by late afternoon and deliver their priceless cargo.

The museum's treasures include beautifully detailed carvings of stone, wood, horn, and bone; painted, quilled, and beaded hide clothing; magnificent examples of Native pottery and basketweaving; and one of the finest collections Navajo textiles in the world. They encompass thousands upon thousands of archaeological objects from Central and South America and the Caribbean; brilliantly hued feather decorations collected from the peoples of the Amazon; beautiful clothing and intricate

ARCHITECTURAL DETAIL of the entrance to the Cultural Resources Center.

walrus-ivory carvings from Inuit communities in Canada. Scholars regard the museum's collections of Native art and artifacts as among the most comprehensive and significant in the world.

How did the museum's holdings reach such proportions? Remarkably enough, the vast majority of them are the legacy of the lifelong passion—some would say obsession—of a single man, George Gustav Heye. Heye has been described as a "boxcar" collector, rather than a connoisseur. In a tribute published by the Museum of the American Indian–Heye Foundation in 1958, a year after Heye's death, his colleagues described his annual trips to favorite places in New Mexico, Arizona, and California. "Don't expect any shipments," he would tell the MAI staff as he set off by train or in one of his limousines. "I'm just going to visit old friends." They knew better.

"In about two weeks after Heye's leave taking," the curator J. Alden Mason wrote, "brief notes would alert the Museum of the imminent arrival of 'a few little things.' These alarms would continue in increasing number, and then the crates, cases, cartons, and barrels would begin to arrive." Heye loved the objects in the collections as much as he enjoyed acquiring them. A debonair and larger-than-life figure, on occasion he decked himself out in Native regalia from the collections, a practice that didn't conform to professional standards for museums even then, much less today. Perhaps it is not surprising—it certainly was not intended to offend anyone—that his nickname among his staff was "the Chief."

It's difficult to grasp the scale of Heye's collecting. He bought his first piece, a Navajo shirt, in 1897, when he was twenty-three. Between that year and 1916, when he established his museum at Audubon Terrace in upper Manhattan, he acquired more than 400,000 objects (a rate of nearly 400 a week). There was space at Audubon Terrace to exhibit only a small proportion of Heye's collections. The majority of objects were kept in storage—initially at his mother's house, then in his own apartment and rented spaces,

RICH IN symbolism, the CRC is designed to be a home for the museum's collections, as well as a center for conservation and research.

and finally, after 1926, at the Research Branch in Pelham Bay, in the very northernmost reaches of the Bronx.

The sheer number of things in the collections stunned researchers and other people fortunate enough to visit the Research Branch. I remember my own first impressions of that rather forbidding building. A maze of dark corridors led to rooms filled with aisle after aisle of floor-to-ceiling shelves holding hundreds—sometimes thousands—of baskets, pots, carvings, garments, masks, toys, boats, and on and on. Every conceivable space was used. There is no denying the romance of the Research Branch—it was quite possible to get lost among the objects there. But it is equally true that, in recent years, academics and Native cultural leaders grew concerned about the wisdom of storing an irreplaceable cultural resource in such an outdated building. When the legislation governing the transfer of the Heye collections to the Smithsonian and establishing the National Museum of the American Indian was written, it also mandated construction of a state-of-the-art research and storage facility at the Smithsonian's Suitland compound, east of Washington.

To appreciate the museum's new Cultural Resources Center, it is important to know that, for many Native people, objects are not inanimate. They are literally alive, and must be sheltered and nourished as living beings. Native and non-Native people who took part in consultations about the design of the museum's programs and facilities envisioned the CRC as a place where the work of curators and conservators would be fully compatible with Native beliefs and observances. Objects would be protected and made accessible to researchers. Equally important, however, the collections would be open to Native communities, cultural authorities, and spiritual figures, so that Native visitors could connect with the objects of their heritage and provide them with traditional care.

The CRC's design embodies this philosophy and links the building symbolically to the natural world. The building's spiral roof is inspired by the geometry of a nautilus shell. A spider's web of small steel beams comes together in a skylight over the center of the rotunda. Inside, directly below the skylight, four glass bricks set in the mahogany floor create a symbolic opening, a reference to those tribes who believe they emerged from the earth. A contemporary fountain runs along the walk to the center's east-facing entrance, and a footbridge leads from the building to a deeply wooded ceremonial circle.

George Horse Capture (A'aninin), senior counselor to the director of NMAI, explains that the architecture of the center reflects concerns discussed during the consultations, especially the principle that the building should "pay the proper respect to the materials" entrusted to it. Horse Capture says that Native people's wishes for this place are summed up in a prayer stick given to the center by Ferrell Secakuku. Secakuku, a former chairman of the Hopi tribe, explained that the feathers on his offering carry prayers for the CRC and were chosen to represent, "Happy home, good luck, and safety." Staff members describe the CRC as the heart and soul of the museum, a place where the collections are at peace.

Construction of the CRC started in 1996 and was completed in the fall of 1998. Six months later, the museum began moving the collections. Inventory technology similar to that used by American manufacturers and retailers helped the staff track objects through the move process. As each pot, shirt, basket, stone point—the list could go on indefinitely—was removed from its shelf at the Research Branch, it was tagged with a bar code representing its catalogue number. Research Branch staff members were also given individual bar-code stickers for their Smithsonian ID cards, enabling scanners to record who worked with each object.

After being tagged and entered into the inventory system, every piece was

EARLY SKETCHES of the CRC reveal the architects' concern with synthesizing program elements and cultural references, such as the east-facing entrance and the circular welcoming area at the center of the spiral roof. The scale of the building, which was designed to accommodate the museum's vast collections, is not at all evident from the entrance.

stabilized, to ensure that it would withstand the rigors of transport. Conservator Emily Kaplan explains:

A more extensive conservation treatment would involve aesthetics as well. Things don't have to be clean or look great in order to be moved. They just have to stay together in one piece so that they arrive safely at the Cultural Resources Center. Once they arrive, safe and sound, they are re-examined and further work can be done. For example, a stabilization treatment for beadwork with broken threads might involve simply tying off the ends of the threads so that beads don't slip off while the object is being moved. A more extensive treatment might involve cleaning the beads, and perhaps restringing loose beads.

After being stabilized, objects were moved on carts to a digital imaging station where they were photographed with their bar codes clearly visible, and the photographs were entered in a database. As the move progressed, staff members could type a catalogue number into the database, call up a digital image of an object, and determine where it was at that moment and who had handled it along the way.

Next, objects were carefully wrapped and packed in boxes. Because boxes often held more than one object, they too were assigned individual bar codes. Boxes were then placed into large, specially designed crates, which the staff called "kivas," after the ceremonial spaces built by Pueblo communities. Each kiva might weigh up to 1,500 pounds, and a truck could carry as many as forty-eight kivas.

A few objects presented special challenges. How, for example, should the team move Heye's Northwest Coast totem poles and house posts, some of which weighed 2,000 pounds and stood eighteen feet high? How, for that matter, did earlier staff get these things into the Research Branch building in

VISITING THE BRONX Research Branch was, in some ways, like traveling back to an era when Americans believed that Native nations would disappear, to be survived only by their material culture. Shelves of stone pestles, collected in California, third floor (archaeology), NMAI Research Branch, 2002. *New York City.*

the first place? A little research revealed that the totem poles and house posts had been brought into the building through windows that have since been bricked over. To move them out, the staff rigged the elevator with steel scaffolding and I-beams, then used an electric winch to lower the totem poles and house posts down the elevator shaft.

As trucks arrived at the Cultural Resources Center, the process was reversed. Boxes were unpacked and objects checked in, examined again to ensure that they had made the trip safely, then taken to their permanent storage spaces. NMAI Collections Manager Pat Nietfeld compares the activity around the arrival of a shipment to working at an archaeological dig: "Each thing on the truck might have been wonderful, but we didn't have time to spend six months or even a week with something. It was a massive quantity of material, and we had to devise ways of making it safe. Every object is different. So it was a question of balancing speed and efficiency with complete respect for the objects."

Two years into the move, I watched the arrival of a shipment in Maryland—no small privilege given the security surrounding the move project. An assistant coordinator in contact with the driver via two-way radio announced that the truck was fifteen minutes away from the CRC. Right on schedule, an unmarked van rolled into the parking lot and slowly backed up to the loading dock. Staff wielding electronic scanners and computer lists began to inventory the shipment. It took about an hour to log forty-five kivas and move them into the collections area. In the morning, the unpacking began. "This is the opportunity to really see this collection as it goes by us," Nietfeld advised me. "Nobody is ever going to have this chance again." Inside the CRC building, the staff grouped ethnographic objects by culture or tribe. Modular shelving makes it possible to organize objects this way, a boon for scholars and community leaders visiting the collections. Archaeological pieces, whose cultural origins are less clear, are grouped geographically by where they were found.

ACQUIRING OBJECTS en masse, Heye created one of the most valuable research collections in the world. Drawer filled with wooden figures, Southwest vault, NMAI Research Branch, 2003. *New York City.*

Many objects in the collections require traditional or ceremonial care. Whenever possible, this is provided by cultural authorities from the relevant tribe during visits to the CRC. During the move, however, staff members often came forward to speak the appropriate words. On the day I was at the CRC, before the truck was unloaded, museum specialist Terry Snowball (Ho-Chunk/Prairie Band Potawatomi) conducted a traditional welcoming ceremony. He addressed the objects softly in Potawatomi. Later, he explained that he had asked for their forgiveness, "forgiveness in touching them and taking care of them, and also for them to have good thoughts about us." After he spoke, Snowball performed a smudging, a rite observed by many

Native cultures on different occasions. He lit a bundle of sage in a large abalone shell and walked to the truck, sweeping the smoke from the burning sage into the open cargo door with an eagle feather. The rest of us had formed a semicircle around him and the van, and when he finished smudging the objects, he gently propelled the sage smoke toward each of us. In this way we were cleansed and reminded of the importance of our work. "In

communities, objects or groups of objects are smudged because they are asking to be smudged," he told me. "Once objects are here, we leave that responsibility to recognized tribal authorities. From what I understand, objects are approached in a good way and left in a good way, sort of like making the way clear, sanctifying it, or purifying it."

Clayton Old Elk (Crow) has visited the Cultural Resources Center many times since he and his family moved from Montana to the Washington area in 1991. At the request of the museum's staff, Old Elk has conducted blessings in both New York and Suitland:

Going into the Cultural Resources Center is like going into a church, because there are sacred objects here. Some of these sacred objects are here by choice, some are not. Some have spiritual connections. For me, it has been a high honor to be involved in the transfer of objects from the Bronx to the Cultural Resources Center. Some of the things that I saw, we still use. The objects here are—maybe—from the past, but still very much current in our practices back home. I am very comfortable with that. At the same time, it is a sad occasion, because some of these things have been lost to us.

I've also had the opportunity to observe how others are handling the objects in a respectful way. They know these objects have been valuable to some people at one time.

There is a good feeling at the Cultural Resources Center. The facility at the Bronx was a real "old school" building. Some of the things were ruined over the years. I saw that as well. Now the objects are being well cared for.

Within the CRC, storage facilities have been modified to accommodate objects that require traditional care. Staff members have replaced metal panels in drawers and cabinet doors with muslin cloth that allows objects to breathe. Muslin is also used to shield powerful or sensitive objects from view.

NATIVE VISITORS to the museum's collections often react with mixed emotions: awe for their ancestors' creativity, sorrow for the loss to communities that collecting represents. Lower pottery area, NMAI Research Branch, 2002. *New York City.*

A WALKWAY leads from the rotunda to a secluded space on the grounds. There Native elders bless the collections and perform ceremonies important to the objects' care.

Native cultural leaders who visit the CRC sometimes leave water and traditional foods—for example, cornmeal or pollen from some of the Southwest tribes, salmon from the Makah people of the Northwest—as sustenance for objects that are very much alive to them. After all, Emily Kaplan observes, "The objects are going to be here for a very long time."

The relationship between museums and the people whose cultural inheritance these institutions hold has evolved since George Heye bought his first hide shirt. At the turn of the twentieth century, many non-Native people perceived Native cultures to be exotic, and Native people to be fundamentally different from themselves. Many non-Native Americans believed, sometimes wistfully, that Indians would soon be extinct. In truth, by that time the Native population of the United States had plunged to an estimated quarter million souls—a tiny fraction of the numbers who were here before European contact. Perhaps we should not be surprised that Heye's collections, like those of many museums, included Native grave objects and human skeletal remains.

From its establishment in 1989—a year before passage of the Native American Graves Protection and Repatriation Act, and two years before the Smithsonian's National Museum of Natural History established a Repatriation Office—NMAI has adhered to a policy of returning human remains and funerary objects, religious and ceremonial artifacts, and communally owned tribal property to individual descendants or tribal groups who can demonstrate their cultural affiliation with the objects and their claim to them. Other culturally sensitive objects, including archival photographs, are used by the museum only with the approval of the appropriate tribes. These principles, controversial when they were adopted, have strengthened the relationships on which the museum's work depends.

In 2000 Alan Pard (Piikani), a traditional spiritualist, took part in the repatriation of objects from the collections to his people on the Peigan

Reserve in Brocket, Alberta. "What we treasured were the sacred items that were given to us from above. We focused our attention on getting back that material," he said. "The white people are the ones who took those things from us, and they should be responsible for their return." Today, Pard describes his experience at the museum as warm and positive. Museum staff welcomed him, listened to him respectfully, and participated in the ceremonies he conducted. During his stay, he delivered blessings at the Research Branch and the CRC to "raise the comfort level" of museum staff members who were working with the collections every day:

The staff wanted some kind of assurance from a spiritual perspective. They were uneasy about moving some of the sacred objects, so they asked me to help on the spiritual side—to help assure them things would be okay. So I came out to the Research Branch, and they explained how they were proceeding to move some of the sacred objects. They were doing everything they could with what they had available—there was a lot of professionalism and respect for the objects.

I can understand why this move was necessary after seeing the Bronx building, which is like a box. There are better facilities now, the building is more spacious, and there are some really sophisticated abilities for storage. I was impressed with the lengths they were going to.

Moving the collections to the CRC was a once-in-a-lifetime undertaking for the museum and its staff. Seeing that the objects are being well cared for spiritually as well as physically, and making them available to Native communities and caregivers, as well as Native and non-Native scholars, is an ongoing commitment. NMAI Director Rick West makes the importance of this effort very clear:

I'm not sure that anyone else in the museum world will ever be put through an exercise like our recent move. I'm not sure it will ever be repeated elsewhere. What I think has relevance, however, is what happens at the NMAI with respect to the care and handling of the objects.

The era when museums could remove and withhold vast amounts of Native material cultural patrimony has come to an end. Museum collections relating to contemporary religious and ceremonial life are becoming

THE METALWORK of the CRC's skylight casts a spider's web of light and shadow on the floor of the welcoming area.

a part of Native communities again. With respect to cultural material not repatriated, we must take the initiative in making objects accessible to the peoples who still use them as an integral part of their lives.

Our success in responding to the perspectives of Native peoples will ultimately benefit all visitors by giving them a fuller, richer, more genuine experience of the collections. Even more important, sharing our collections and the scholarship associated with them with Native communities contributes, in significant ways, to the continuation of vital elements of American culture.

CHAPTER FIVE

New York City in Indian Possession

THE GEORGE GUSTAV HEYE CENTER

by John Haworth

On September 11, 2001, when the first plane struck the World Trade Center, I was just outside the George Gustav Heye Center, six blocks from the twin towers, thinking about an important meeting scheduled later in the day. As the terrible events of that morning followed one upon another, I'm proud to say that the museum staff acted quickly to safeguard the valuable collections and works of art on exhibit in our galleries. Facility managers and maintenance staff shut off the ventilation system, to keep smoke and dust from infiltrating the building. And people began trying to locate every colleague on the museum's staff, as well as our board members and volunteers—an effort that continued for the next few days. In the end, we were lucky: everyone was safe. That morning, as I joined tens of thousands of other stunned and heartbroken people making our way out of lower Manhattan on foot, I couldn't help but think of the Long Walks many of our forebears made.

As the enormity of what had happened became known, the world mourned with New York. Empathy may be a universal human reaction to such profound grief. But I also believe people see

MOHAWK IRONWORKERS. (From left to right) Benji Roundpoint, Dick Otto, and Mike Schlinder, ca. 2000. *New York City.*

this city, one of the great cultural capitals of our time, as a place in which we all have a stake.

It was New York's standing as a center of the arts that brought me here. I was born in the red-clay country of western Oklahoma and grew up in northeastern Oklahoma, not far from the childhood home of Rick West, forty years later the founding director of the National Museum of the American Indian. I didn't know Rick then, but my parents bought one of his father's paintings. My mother and father were supportive of the Five Tribes Museum in Muskogee during its early days and were interested in the work of Indian artists. Dick West, Rick's father, was already revered throughout Oklahoma and beyond for his art, for the many painters whose work he fought to see recognized, and for his strong belief in the value of Indian cultures. I remember standing beside the pump on my paternal grandmother's farm with Mr. West while my father took a snapshot of us.

That farm nestled in the Arkansas River bottoms. The land had been allotted to our family when the U.S. Congress dissolved the tribal governments and parceled out communal lands to individual Indians in preparation for the Oklahoma Territory to become a state. My Indian upbringing, such as it was, came from my grandmother, a woman who moved quietly and with perfect calm in the background of our rather rowdy family, and from our pride in Earl Boyd Pierce, my father's first cousin and the tribal counsel for the Western Cherokee Nation throughout most of my childhood. Earl's fight for the tribe to receive payment for sand removed from the Arkansas River bed, a legal struggle that reached all the way to the Supreme Court, formed part of our family's consciousness. Indeed, trucks carrying the stolen sand sometime ran us off to the side of the section-line road. As for my own place in the Cherokee community, I rode on my grandmother and Earl's coattails.

My interests were in the arts. A generation earlier, Dick West and other artists,

THE CUSTOM HOUSE, its architecture trumpeting America's place in the world, makes a grand stage for a museum that celebrates the Western Hemisphere's original peoples.

including Maria Tallchief and a remarkable group of Native American ballerinas, had staked Oklahoma's claim to a place in America's art galleries and concert halls. After receiving a degree in music from the University of Oklahoma—which retired its Indian mascot, "Little Red," during my tenure there—I had the good fortune to receive a year-long internship from the National Endowment for the Arts to develop cultural programming in Oklahoma.

When that internship ended in 1973, I accepted a position with the Arizona Arts and Humanities Commission. While I was there, I helped coordinate a tour by the newly established Native American Theatre

Ensemble to Native and non-Native communities throughout the state. The ensemble's work very naturally reflected a strong Native perspective, and I still remember listening to people active in the Scottsdale cultural scene worry about how the audience might react to something as

THE IMMENSE arch of the elliptical rotunda, built according to the principles of Spanish-immigrant engineer Rafael Guastavino, supports a skylight that weighs 140 tons.

provocative as the ensemble's production of the Pocahontas story.

During a summer studying arts administration at Harvard, I made some friends at the National Council for the Arts, and one of them encouraged me to apply for an opening on the staff of the New York State Council for the Arts. And so, in my mid-twenties, I moved to New York City. Among the going-away presents my grandmother gave me was a subscription to the *Cherokee Advocate,* Indian Territory's oldest newspaper and an institution to a Native nation that prides itself on its history of written language. That subscription was my grandmother's way of asking me not to forget my home. Oddly enough one of the most famous newspapers of our time greeted me on my arrival in New York: the October 30, 1975, *New York Daily News* with the headline, "Ford to City: Drop Dead," summarizing Washington's refusal to save the city from near-bankruptcy.

For the next twenty years, I worked with community-based cultural organizations, from grassroots groups to major institutions, first with the State Council for the Arts and eventually with the city's Department of Cultural Affairs. From those vantage points, I followed the long process of negotiation that ultimately dissolved the Heye Foundation and established the National Museum of the American Indian within the Smithsonian.

I remember a few things in particular from that time. One is the importance to many New Yorkers of the old Museum of the American Indian, a fixture in the memory of everyone who ever visited it as a child. Another is the very genuine bipartisan support for the creation of the Heye Center in New York, as well as for the new museum on the National Mall. Senator Daniel Patrick Moynihan played a key role in the ambitious conception of the new museum, of course. Yet it was President Ronald Reagan who agreed, after a visit to the city in 1985, to lease space in the Alexander Hamilton U.S. Custom House to the museum for ninety-nine years at a nominal rent of one dollar per year. Barber Conable, who had recently retired from the Wyoming seat in the House of Representatives, asked David Rockefeller to raise that possibility with the president. One of Rockefeller's assistants later said that the idea seemed to appeal to the president's sense of himself as a man of the Old West. (New York's other senator, Alphonse D'Amato, opposed the magnanimous gesture, calling Reagan's trip "the costliest visit a president ever paid to New York.")

The other thing that impressed me at the time, and still impresses me, is the good faith of the Heye Foundation Board of Trustees, who recognized the tremendous research value of the Heye collections and were committed to finding a way to keep them intact. Securing the collections' future must have been a bittersweet achievement for them. I am grateful to the many members of that board who support the museum in its new incarnation, especially Julie Johnson Kidd, who as chairman of the Heye Foundation in 1989 signed the agreement transferring the collections to the Smithsonian and who has continued to serve the museum.

I joined the museum staff in 1995, a year after the Heye Center opened in the beautifully restored Custom House. The southern tip of Manhattan,

MY LOVE, Miss Liberty, 1987. Doll made by Rosalie Paniyak (Cup'ik Eskimo).
Chevak, Alaska. Indian Arts and Crafts Board Collection, Department of the Interior, at NMAI. 25/5563

PRECEDING PAGES: The exterior of the Custom House covers three square blocks in lower Manhattan. The four large sculptures along the main façade—female figures representing America, Asia, Europe, and Africa—are by Daniel Chester French, the artist who created the statue of Abraham Lincoln for the Lincoln Memorial in Washington.

best known as the center of the financial world, has turned out to be a very appropriate site for an Indian museum. Evidence of Native influence and American history abounds here. Broadway, after all, follows the Wiechquaekeck Trail, an old Algonquian trade route that continued north along the Hudson River. Across the street from the Custom House, in historic Battery Park, stands a monument dedicated to Native American trade with the Dutch. Here in 1626, legend has it, Peter Minuit purchased Manhattan from a band of Canarsie Indians for sixty guilders' worth of trinkets and beads.

In his classic satire about the history of the United States, comedian Stan Freberg imagines the Indians of Manhattan closing their deal with the Dutch, then striking the forest like a stage set to reveal that the whole island is actually paved. "Nice place to visit," Freberg's Indians tell the Dutch, "but you really wouldn't want to live here." In fact, many scholars have argued that Native understandings would have led the Canarsie to believe that they were granting the Dutch limited land use, rather than ownership. Whatever the circumstances of the exchange, it represents a pivotal moment in the region's history. In *New York City in Indian Possession*, a monograph on Indian deeds, colonial charters, and other land transactions in this area

published by the Heye Foundation in 1920, local authority Reginald Pelham Bolton describes the importance of the Dutch foothold:

> [T]he settlement which certain Indians permitted to take on the lower end of Manhattan became of vital importance to the intruding race by its geographical situation, its central and secure position, and its easy access by water, north, south, and east. Once in possession of that defensible point, the white man could not be dislodged, and while his settlements elsewhere were more or less defenseless, and were destroyed at one time or other, the New Amsterdam site was never seriously threatened with extermination.

The "wall" of Wall Street, five blocks north of the Heye Center, refers to the barricade constructed by the Dutch to protect their settlements from Indian incursions. Until 1790, Minuit's Fort Amsterdam stood on the land now occupied by the Custom House. That year, the state legislature commissioned the construction on this site of Government House, a grand, red-brick home for the U.S. president, in a failed bid to win George Washington's support for New York as the new nation's capital.

Today, New York City is developing Battery Park as an important cultural destination. As I look around the neighborhood, I'm struck by the fact that the Heye Center presents the stories of the people who were first here, while institutions nearby—the Statue of Liberty and the Ellis Island Immigration Museum in the harbor, the Museum of Jewish Heritage, and the Irish Hunger Memorial, among others—tell the stories of the people who came later.

The Custom House, designed by architect Cass Gilbert and opened in 1907, is a landmark in its own right—one of New York's most lavish Beaux Arts buildings and a high point of the City Beautiful movement of the turn

DEPRESSION-ERA painter Reginald Marsh and eight assistants produced two series of murals for the Rotunda. One series depicts early explorers of the Americas. The second, which includes the panel opposite, traces the course of a ship entering New York Harbor.

THIS FAMOUS photograph, taken in 1932, includes at least three Mohawk ironworkers from Kahnawake Reserve, Quebec: Peter Skaronhiati Stacey (third from left), Joseph Jocks (fourth from left), and Peter Sakaronhiotane Rice (sixth from left).
Rockefeller Center, New York City.

of the twentieth century. Before the widespread imposition of the income tax, import duties provided the bulk of the nation's revenue, and New York was one of America's most lucrative ports. Every detail of the architecture of the Custom House—from Daniel Chester French's dramatic limestone sculptures depicting the continents to the murals that decorate the rotunda, commissioned by the Treasury Relief Art Project and painted in dry fresco by Reginald Marsh—speaks to America's image of itself as great power taking its destined place in the world.

SPIRIT OF A NATIVE PLACE

Rick West and others have already described in this book the ways in which the museum's principles and mission guide our work. Since the Heye Center opened in 1994, our staff has worked to put these ideals into practice through exhibitions, symposia and other public programs, outreach to new audiences, and alliances with Native communities and institutions. I'll give only a few examples, although there are many more.

All Roads Are Good, one of the Heye Center's three inaugural exhibitions, on view from 1994 through 2000, presented objects from the museum's collections chosen and interpreted by Native people from throughout the Western Hemisphere. Twenty-three Native artists and cultural leaders were invited to the museum's Research Branch in the Bronx to make selections from the collections, then asked to describe in their own words why this cultural patrimony is important to them and how it reflects their cultural realities. The central installation from that exhibition, moccasins from throughout Native America arranged in a dance circle by artist and curator Gerald McMaster (Plains Cree), now Rick West's special assistant for Mall exhibitions, has become one of the museum's enduring images.

MOCCASINS arranged for the Heye Center inaugural exhibition *All Roads Are Good.*

In 1996 the Heye Center produced *Woven by the Grandmothers: Nineteenth Century Navajo Textiles from the National Museum of the American Indian,* an exhibition based on an eight-year collaboration, begun by the late Eulalie Bonar when she was a curator at the Museum of the American Indian, with Navajo weavers D. Y. Begay, Wesley Thomas, and Kalley Keams. Many more weavers took part in a related workshop at the Navajo Community College in Tsaile, Arizona, where they were invited to study textiles from the museum's outstanding collections. The exhibition was also shown at cultural centers in six Central and South American countries under the auspices of the White House Millennium Program and the U.S. Department of State.

In 2002 *The Edge of Enchantment* explored the indigenous communities of coastal Oaxaca, Mexico, and the ways in which their history, land tenure, and spiritual beliefs are interwoven. This exhibition, too, was the product of years of collaboration between the curator, Alicia González, and the people of the towns and villages she portrayed. After being shown in New York and Oaxaca City, photographs and other materials from the exhibition were returned to the people of the region, along with copies of the curator's original research. These materials are being used to help establish two new community museums in Huatulco and Huamelula.

Closer to home, we are working with local partners. In the 2000 census, more than 87,000 New Yorkers describe themselves as American Indians or Alaska Natives. This surprising number makes New York home to the largest urban Indian population in the country. My colleagues and I are committed to seeing that the Heye Center serves this community.

That brings me back to the events of 2001. On September 19, eight days after the Trade Center fell, Clinton Elliott (Ojibwe), a member of the Heye Center staff, performed a blessing ceremony to welcome us back to the Custom House. Later that fall, shortly before Thanksgiving, Jerry Flute, a former chairman of the Sisseton/Wahpeton Sioux Tribe, and Henrietta Mann (Southern Cheyenne), chair of Native American Studies at Montana State University and a member of the museum's board, conducted a traditional Wiping of the Tears Ceremony at the Heye Center. Judges from the federal courts that share the Custom House with us, Wall Street clerks and traders, residents of the neighborhoods of lower Manhattan, and colleagues from other cultural institutions joined us in helping to release the souls of the dead, and with them some of our own sorrow. The ceremony reminded us that we would survive and move forward. For me, it also showed how deeply committed Native people are to healing, and to the idea of community.

HOOP DANCER Derrick Davis (Hopi/Choctaw) performing at the opening of the Heye Center, 1994.

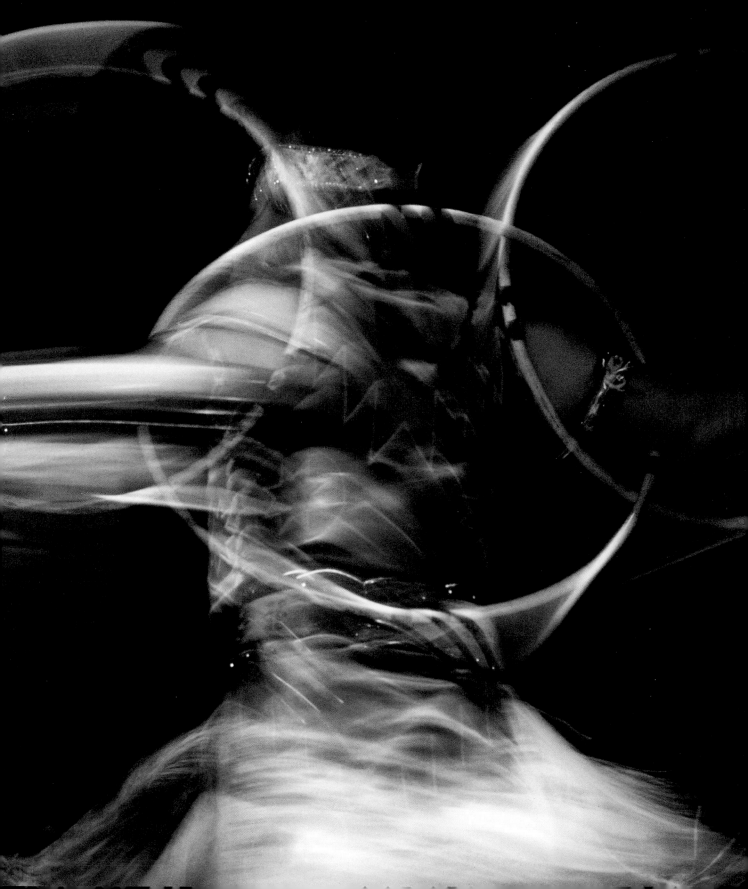

Soon after the Heye Center reopened, we noticed that several Native American ironworkers had begun walking down from the Trade Center site to visit the museum. Mohawk ironworkers helped to build New York's bridges and skyscrapers, including the Empire State Building and the World Trade Center. Now, Mohawk workmen had returned to help clean up the wreckage of 9/11.

The Heye Center staff decided that we'd like to create a photography exhibition acknowledging these workers' historic contributions. *Booming Out: Mohawk Ironworkers Build New York* explored the history and achievements of ironworkers from Akwesasne, on the border between Ontario and New York State, and Kahnawake, near Montreal. (During the mid-twentieth century, the Boerum Hill neighborhood of Brooklyn, site of Ironworkers Union Local 361, was nicknamed "Downtown Kahnawake" by the many Mohawk skilled laborers who divided their time between jobs in the city and families up north.) In conjunction with the exhibition, which opened in April 2002, the ironworkers spoke to a packed house about their work at the Trade Center site and their families and communities back home. They described how their experiences at ground zero had already changed their lives, and they presented the museum with a sculpture of the twin towers welded from materials salvaged from the rubble.

In 1998, NMAI published *Coyote in Love with a Star,* a children's book by Marty Kreipe de Montaño (Prairie Band Potawatomi), with illustrations by Tom Coffin (Prairie Band Potawatomi/Creek). In the book, Marty, the manager of museum's Resource Center and for many years a resident of New York, imagines Coyote, lonely and broke on the Potawatomi Reservation in Kansas, deciding to set out "toward the place where the sun comes up" to look for a job in New York.

Everything about the city is new to Coyote—the ethnic neighborhoods, the crowded sidewalks, the tall buildings, the subway—but he finds work "in his field" as rodent control officer at the World Trade Center. There, "on clear nights, Coyote would escape the noise and hurry of the city by going up to the observation deck to watch the stars as they danced across the sky.

"Once, when the stars came very close, he noticed one star that was more beautiful than all the rest. She was so beautiful that Coyote fell in love with her."

It's difficult to read of Coyote's longing, or to look at Tom Coffin's illustrations of the Trade Center, without experiencing a profound sense of loss. For the last few years, we have invited the public to the Heye Center for a reading of Marty's modern fable as part of our commemoration of September 11.

Nearly 400 years ago, within steps of the Heye Center, the representatives of two Old Worlds met. Peter Minuit had great ambitions for the settlement he named New Amsterdam. The Canarsie Indians, on the other hand, assumed that their people would always continue to make a life for themselves on this land and its waterways. In the end, both were right. The people who were first here are still here, helping to build and rebuild one of our civilization's great cities.

A POTAWATOMI fable transported to New York, *Coyote in Love with a Star* has become one of the museum's most popular children's books. It speaks to the yearning that characterizes human existence, whether we live on isolated reservations or in big cities.

"A Most Beautiful Sight Presented Itself to My View"

THE LONG RETURN TO A NATIVE PLACE ON THE MALL

by Douglas E. Evelyn

Extending from the foot of the U.S. Capitol to the Potomac River lies a beautiful open space we call by a number of different names—the Washington Mall, the National Mall, America's Front Yard. The Mall has long been a stage for the nation's iconic museums and memorials, and for the celebrations and protests that remind us of, and help define, our freedom. In September 2004, the Smithsonian Institution's National Museum of the American Indian opened here, dedicated to restoring the stories, experiences, and aspirations of the first peoples of this land to their place in American history, and to sharing something of what it means to be Indian with millions of people who visit what is now, again, a Native place.

The creation of the National Mall has not been painless, and no portion of it has been more hotly contested than the east end, the site of the new museum. Even as the final disposition of the site was delayed and debated over the past two centuries, the nation's first Americans strived to sustain their cultures and to be recognized as full partners in American society. Now these struggles have converged in a living museum that will

THE NATIONAL MUSEUM of the American Indian and the U.S. Capitol.

View from National-Monument, looking East.   Washington, D. C.

POSTCARD LOOKING east on the National Mall, 1900. Romantic landscapes dominate the Mall, surrounding the Smithsonian Castle and the original Agriculture Department buildings. Note the intrusive railroad shed and tracks at the upper left, separating the east end from the rest of the Mall.

celebrate the survival and ongoing vitality of Native cultures.

Washington's setting, where the Piedmont Plateau meets the Coastal Plain, has always been beautiful, with low hills rising westward toward the Appalachian Mountains and the grand Potomac leading eastward to the Atlantic. The Great Falls of the Potomac, upriver from Washington, dramatically mark the shift from plateau to plain, while the meandering Anacostia River, once called the Eastern Branch, frames the city on the southeast. Rock Creek divides the northwest section of town and defines one of the nation's oldest and loveliest urban parks. Smaller streams once abounded here, the most prominent coursing past what has become Capitol Hill. At about where the National Museum of the American Indian stands, this stream—called Goose Creek and then Tiber Creek—turned north and then west, broadening gradually as it merged with the Potomac. The creek mediated between hills and lowlands, fresh water and ocean, land and sky. Its natural, sometimes violent, effects gradually shaped the marshy (some said swampy) land.

Long before Europeans arrived, Native Americans lived here. A map drawn in 1612 by John Smith, who had founded the European settlement at Jamestown, Virginia, five years before, shows Algonquian villages on both sides of the Potomac. Two villages were within the area now occupied by the District of Columbia, one, whose name is no longer known, west of Georgetown, and another, Nacochtanke, along the east bank of the Anacostia River, a prominent site of Native settlements over the centuries.

Also within the current District limits were several Native sites for meeting, fishing, and quarrying. Evidence of Indian presence has been unearthed along the Potomac near Chain Bridge, downstream from the Maryland state line; along the west side of Connecticut Avenue near Van Ness, in midtown; and on and near the Mall, including, in the late 1800s,

LOOKING WEST from the Capitol, 1868. The city intrudes on the Mall. Gasworks (smokestacks, upper left) stand on what is now NMAI's site.

on the grounds of the Washington Monument. In 1975 excavations for the White House swimming pool exposed projectile points and pottery fragments, and ceramics and other items were uncovered the next year on the nearby Ellipse. No Native American artifacts have been found at the Indian museum's site, but clearly Natives lived throughout the area.

The European-American history of the museum site largely begins in 1632, when England's King Charles I granted the request of the late Cecil Calvert, Lord Baltimore, to provide a haven for persecuted Catholics in the American colonies. Baltimore's sons Cecil and Leonard began establishing settlements

THOMAS JEFFERSON and James Madison discuss the site of the future capital. Undated illustration.

and granting large tracts of land in Maryland to various favorites, including George Thompson, court clerk of Charles County, who in 1663 received three parcels totaling 1,800 acres. The property descended through the Carroll family and eventually was acquired by the federal government for the District of Columbia. What is today the site of the museum was described in a 1790 survey as "Mr. Carroll's part of Duddington Pasture."

Up to that time, the U.S. government had met in eight different cities. Among its most pressing concerns was creating a permanent capital, which the Constitution had stipulated in 1787 would be within a federal district of up to ten miles square. The most populous states were in the north, and the nation's temporary capitals had been in New York, Pennsylvania, New Jersey, and Maryland. Powerful forces argued for a more southerly location, more central to the direction in which the founders believed the nation would grow. By spring 1790, the choice had been narrowed to Philadelphia, the most prominent city of the time, and Georgetown, Maryland, a tobacco port on the Potomac that linked commercial ocean routes with the projected populations west of the Appalachians.

Thomas Jefferson, then secretary of state, brokered the resolution of the capital's location at an intimate dinner in about May of that year. The decision grew out of a fight to have the federal government assume debts that states, especially in the northeast, had incurred during the Revolutionary War. Creditor states, mostly in the South, opposed the action in "the most bitter & angry contests ever known in Congress."

When the measure failed in the House of Representatives, the debtor states threatened to secede from the Union. Since his colleague Alexander Hamilton, secretary of the treasury, "was in despair," Jefferson agreed to bring him together with Alexander White and Richard Bland Lee, congressmen from Virginia, in the hope that "reasonable men, consulting together coolly [could] form a compromise . . . to save the union."

PIERRE L'ENFANT laid out a city bounded to the west, south, and east by the waters of Rock Creek, the Potomac, and the Eastern Branch (now the Anacostia River), and to the north by the edge of the Coastal Plain (now Florida Avenue). He assigned sites for the Capitol and President's House, connected by the President's Park (today's Ellipse) and the Mall. Tiber Creek was to be channeled into a canal between the two rivers. Reclamation projects beginning in the 1880s filled the Potomac to the west of the Mall, allowing the Lincoln and Jefferson Memorials to be built along the river.

These reasonable men ultimately concurred that the federal government would absorb the war debts. In addition, Philadelphia would be the site of the capital for ten years, but then, to sweeten the bitter pill for the South, the capital would move to a permanent location on the Potomac near Georgetown. Hamilton convinced the northern delegations to agree, and White and Lee changed their votes. Daniel Carroll, who held large pieces of land in the proposed area, also switched positions and was subsequently appointed one of the commissioners to monitor construction of the new city. The Residence Act of July 1, 1790, made the agreement official.

A larger cast then began to play roles in the new city's evolution. President Washington himself, closely advised by Jefferson, actively oversaw land acquisition, site planning, and design and completion of public buildings. To design the city, Washington chose the most qualified person in the country, Maj. Pierre Charles L'Enfant, a versatile French engineer and designer who had long campaigned for the job.

L'Enfant had volunteered for the American cause in July 1776, within weeks of the Declaration of Independence. By the next summer he was serving under another European, Baron Friedrich von Steuben, at Valley Forge. Even then L'Enfant was called upon for all manner of design work, and he impressed Washington with his artistry as well as his gallantry in battle. L'Enfant illustrated training and drill manuals; depicted military sites; designed insignia, certificates, medals, and monuments to fallen heroes; and planned buildings and official presentations. After the war he undertook numerous assignments in New York City, including remodeling City Hall to create Federal Hall for sessions of the first Federal Congress and Washington's inauguration on April 30, 1789. That September, L'Enfant asked the president to let him plan the proposed federal city and also to appoint him federal engineer, in which position he would fortify harbors and maritime sites. When he took up this new post, on March 9, 1791, surveying and mapping of the federal site on the Potomac was already under way. Secretary of State Jefferson instructed him to proceed from the "eastern branch . . . upwards, laying down the hills, valleys, morasses, and waters between that, the Potomac, the Tyber, and the road leading from Georgetown to the eastern branch," all toward determining the most appropriate "site for the federal town and buildings."

Over several weeks, L'Enfant studied the terrain and the requirements for key buildings, monuments, and architectural features. He reviewed

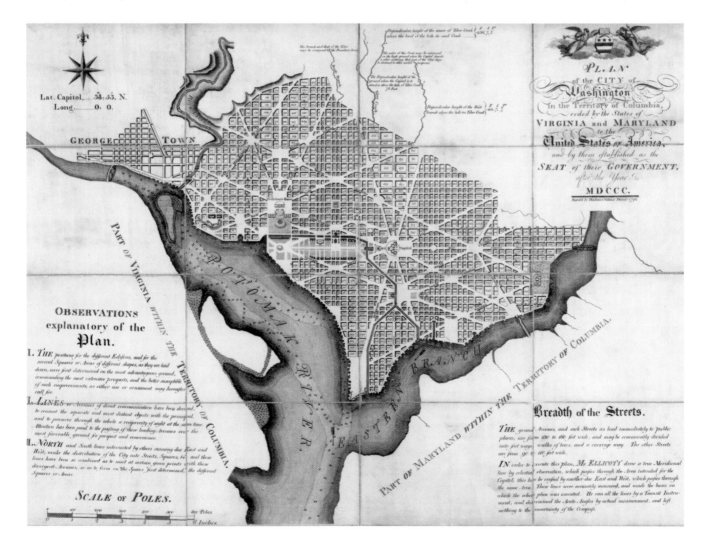

plans of the great cityscapes of Europe, contemplated the capital's economic viability and future growth, and incorporated ideas and designs that would spur investment and allow for expansion. His overall plan was grand in vision and scale, and it continues to work. He placed important buildings for Congress and the president on elevated natural sites, the former on "Jenkins heights which stands as a pedestal waiting for a monument," and the latter "on a ridge [with a view] 10 or 12 miles down the Potowmack." From these two buildings, he projected broad open parks toward the Potomac, now the National Mall and the Ellipse, intersecting at a point reserved for the Washington Monument. Much could be said about other elements of the design—the grand diagonal boulevards superimposed upon a grid of streets, creating circles and intersections that are the bane of automobile drivers—but his vision for the Mall is the focus here. Extending from the base of a cascade, which was never built, down the west terrace of the Capitol, he prescribed a "Grand Avenue, 400 feet in breadth and about a mile in length," a scale without precedent in the American cities of his time.

From the start, there was a tension inherent between L'Enfant's grand ends and the financial means needed to achieve them. Intended to accommodate an eventual population of hundreds of thousands, L'Enfant's plan for the capital exceeded the economic realities of the early local and federal governments, and for decades the Mall remained a low priority. In 1842, after viewing Washington's underdeveloped avenues and spaces, Charles Dickens dubbed it the "City of Magnificent Intentions." In fact, government officials were planning to make improvements to the Mall even as Dickens wrote, though it would not begin to reflect L'Enfant's intentions until well into the twentieth century.

Perhaps the most detailed account of the early Mall is that of Christian Hines, from his *Early Recollections of Washington City*, published in 1866.

Hines remembered being sent as a boy, in about 1797, on an errand to Greenleaf's Point (now Fort McNair). After setting out from Georgetown, and walking past the site of the "President's House" toward "where the Centre Market-house now stands" (Eighth Street and Pennsylvania Avenue, Northwest), he headed south across the Mall near what is now Ninth Street:

> On the east side of the road there were, I suppose, several acres of elegant forest trees. On the west side there were not so many, there being only a narrow strip. I think part, or perhaps all, of them were on the public mall. . . . We then passed through the woods, when a most beautiful sight presented itself to my view, such as I had never seen before. A vast plain of old fields extended southwardly almost as far as my eye could reach, and scarcely anything could be seen on either side but the old mansion, The Twenty Buildings, and a few old farm houses, and once in a while a few fruit trees that formerly belonged to farms.

Hines recalled that the terrain at the east end of the Mall near the Capitol was overgrown and rough, "a complete little wilderness."

Other accounts noted that some portions of the Mall were marshy and some were once forested. On August 12, 1806, Benjamin Henry Latrobe, the surveyor of public buildings and the most versatile architect in America, described "the uninhabited part of town" between the Capitol and the houses south of the Mall, as "a low swampy piece of ground covered with Bushes." The marshes were especially pronounced toward its eastern end. Ten years later, in 1816, U.S. Consul to France David Baillie Warden noted that "Washington has been lately deprived of . . . the spreading shade of magnificent trees. Between the Capitol and the President's

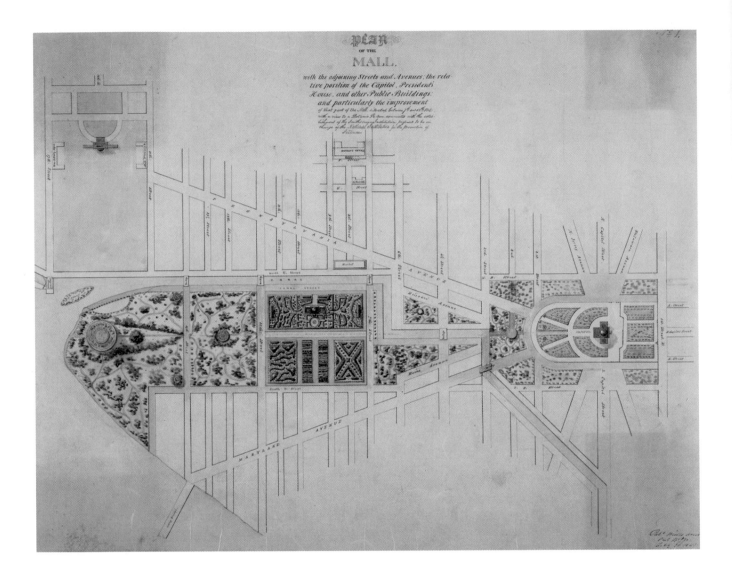

PLAN
OF THE
MALL.
with the adjoining Streets and Avenues; the rela
tive position of the Capitol, Presidents
House, and other Public Buildings:
and particularly the improvement

House, a certain space of thickly-shaded ground extending towards the river, destined for a public walk, was admirably fitted for this purpose; but the oaks and other forest trees with which it was adorned, have been wantonly destroyed." By Warden's time, the Mall had been cleared.

Tiber Creek, the most prominent and unruly natural feature of the Mall, proved far more difficult to control than the trees. Christian Hines described a particularly violent flood in 1802 or 1804, during which Jefferson, by then president, offered rescuers "fifteen dollars for each person saved." L'Enfant's plan called for a canal to channel the Tiber and link the Potomac and Eastern Branch shipping, so that goods could be brought to the center city and market. But funding proved difficult, and it was not until 1815 that the canal was completed. Its route separated the Mall and southern portion of the city into a section referred to as "the Island," limiting the area's access and delaying its development. Even when finished, the canal required constant maintenance and improvements. Tiber Creek overwhelmed it. In 1852 the city planner Robert Mills cited the creek's "ruinous effects . . . [on the canal], destroying its navigation & creating disease and great expense [and a] perpetual drain upon the Treasury." By 1860 the area had become "a canal by name but a municipal sewer by use." Finally, in the 1870s, massive public works projects transformed the landscape, using mountains of soil to fill low areas of the Mall and the canal, and creating Constitution Avenue. Subsequent projects tunneled the Tiber into the Potomac and filled in the eastern end of the canal, forming what is now Washington Avenue, Southwest.

MUSEUMS RISE ON THE MALL

Significantly, a botanical garden was one of the first uses proposed for what is now the site of the museum. Early in the Jefferson administration, Thomas Law petitioned Congress to develop the neglected spaces of the Mall, "now laying waste and neglected to the site," into spaces of "ornament and utility." Law suggested that a botanical garden might be "of essential service to the

ROBERT AND Eliza Mills, ca. 1851 (above). The Mills Plan (opposite), drafted in 1841, projects the development of the Smithsonian as a botanical garden, with adjacent grounds featuring plantings, memorials, and circuitous drives.

Community at large." A decade later, he helped found the Columbian Institute for the Promotion of Science, established to operate a library, museum, and botanical garden. In 1820 Congress set aside five acres for that purpose at the foot of Capitol Hill, and expanded the acreage in 1824. The land was fenced, planted, and opened for public use, and though the institute faded in the 1830s, the area continued to be identified with botanical gardens and public education.

The birth of the Smithsonian ensured the Mall's place as a center for Washington's national museums. In 1826 British scientist James Smithson bequeathed more than $500,000 to the United States—a country he had never seen—to establish in Washington an institution "for the increase and diffusion of knowledge among men." The government learned of the gift in 1835. After a decade of debate about the best use for the bequest, in 1846 Congress established the Smithsonian Institution, consisting of research enterprises, a library, and an art gallery. The sector of the Mall between Seventh and Twelfth Streets was set aside for the new institution and was called the Smithsonian Park.

In addition to James Smithson, a second significant figure in the transformation of the Mall during the first half of the nineteenth century was Robert Mills. Born in Charleston, South Carolina, in 1781, Mills claimed to be the first native-born American architect. He trained in Washington under James Hoban at the Capitol and President's House, made architectural drawings for Thomas Jefferson, and apprenticed during the first decade of the nineteenth century with Benjamin Latrobe, who was then designing the Washington City Canal and completing the city's first generation of public buildings. An expert in fireproof construction, Mills designed all manner of public buildings and monuments—hospitals, courthouses, jails, churches, record centers, and government offices. He was also an engineer, concerning himself with water and transportation systems, and the infrastructure of America's growing cities.

After working on projects in Richmond, Philadelphia, and Baltimore, and for South Carolina's Board of Public Works, Mills lobbied the South Carolina congressional delegation for federal opportunities in Andrew Jackson's administration. In 1830 Mills returned with his family to the city where he had apprenticed. Secure in his American training and determined to produce dignified and useful architecture for his nation's capital, Mills served as the government's principal architect for the next quarter century. By 1840 he was overseeing the largest public works program ever conducted in Washington—the simultaneous construction of the Treasury, Patent Office, and General Post Office buildings, along with lesser projects like the Washington City Jail.

Mills's fellow South Carolinian and sometime patron, Joel R. Poinsett, secretary of war from 1837 to 1841, was determined to establish a national museum in Washington—the National Institution for the Promotion of Science, a successor to the defunct Columbian Institute. At the same time, Poinsett maneuvered to display the collections gathered by the United States Exploring Expedition to the South Pacific (1838–1842) in Mills's newly completed Patent Office. Outflanked, the commissioner of patents found his main gallery, where he'd planned to display American inventions, usurped for all manner of exhibits, including natural history specimens, George Washington's tent and military gear, and portraits of American Indians, which Poinsett had transferred from the War Department. This collection, formed by federal Indian Agency officer Thomas McKenny and originally exhibited in 1818, constituted the first public museum in Washington. The commissioner of patents had to accommodate the national collections for nearly two decades before many of them were transferred to the Smithsonian Institution.

In the final days of the Van Buren administration, Poinsett asked Mills to

THE SMITHSONIAN Institution, seen from 15th and E Streets, Northwest, 1860s. The west end of the Mall and residential neighborhoods of Southwest Washington are separated from downtown by the canal, seen entering the frame at the right. Causeways at 12th Street (background) and 14th Street (midground) lead to the Potomac.

prepare a plan to improve "that part of the Mall . . . between 7th and 12th Sts West for a botanical garden" and for building there the National Institution for the Promotion of Science, potentially to accommodate the Smithsonian Institution. On February 23, 1841, Mills presented his ideas for the building and grounds, including the first comprehensive landscaping plan for the

Mall. The landscape encompassed the canal, market, and Washington Monument, for which Mills had already proposed designs and which he eventually would be commissioned to build.

Mills's landscape plan, with its nineteenth-century romantic sensibility in full bloom, signaled a turning away from the classically elegant openness envisaged by L'Enfant. It included "serpentine walks" and drives among groupings of trees that would provide "a continued variation of the scene . . . for several miles" and permit "picturesque views" of buildings and "objects . . . of a monumental character." Mills's landscape designs were not implemented, because the Democrats, including Poinsett, were replaced, and the National Institution's flame sputtered.

By the end of the 1840s, however, the Smithsonian had been established, independent from the National Institution but intriguingly similar in structure and function. The Castle was under construction in the center of the Mall (with Mills as superintendent), the Washington Monument was rising at what was then the west end, and the Smithsonian was urging the federal government to engage the nation's most prominent landscape designer, Andrew Jackson Downing, to create a new plan for the area.

Downing's plan was more fully developed and comprehensive than Mills's. Besides extensive serpentine walks and drives, it featured six discrete gardens: the Botanic Gardens, Fountain Park (at the center of the Mall between Third and Seventh Streets), the Smithsonian Pleasure Grounds (Seventh to Twelfth Streets), an Evergreen Garden, Monument Park (surrounding the Washington Monument), and the Parade or President's Park (now the Ellipse). Historian Therese O'Malley's study of Downing's plan notes his intentions to create a national park that would improve public taste and appreciation for landscape design while educating visitors about specific types of plants. Downing called his creation "a public museum of living trees and shrubs," with explanatory labels for plants and special emphasis on species that were suited to Washington's climate. Alas, just after completing his plans, tragedy struck down this promising young man: in 1852 Downing drowned trying to rescue victims of a steamboat explosion on the Hudson River. He was thirty-seven.

While never fully implemented, Downing's romantic plans influenced the landscaping of the Mall, and his views advanced former proposals for its educational use. Winding drives and tastefully grouped trees were prominent features of the late-nineteenth century Mall, and the Department of Agriculture's propagating gardens, arboretum, and plant houses—the Agriculture Building opened in 1868 near the Smithsonian Castle—reflected many of Downing's educational themes.

ALONG TIBER CREEK

Taming the east end of the Mall between First and Seventh Streets—the low and marshy land pierced by Tiber Creek—proved daunting. In the late eighteenth and early nineteenth centuries, the public viewed the Mall as a commons, and people often used it on a first-come, first-served basis. Historical records document frequent complaints and petitions concerning squatters, randomly fenced gardens and grazing plots, and dumping.

At that time, the Mall was an unregulated federal reserve, and its east end was in a particularly crucial location near the downtown that was emerging between the Capitol and the President's House. It is perhaps not surprising, then, that soon after setting aside space for the botanical gardens and completing the city canal, officials assigned major sections of the east Mall for urban

THE TRAIL OF TEARS

Because this book concerns the history of the Smithsonian's National Museum of the American Indian, it is relevant to note the impact on mid-nineteenth-century American Indians of the federal government, then also shaping the nation's capital. The same impulse that created the symbols of the nation in Washington—monuments, national museums, and blocks of federal offices—also projected the power of the national government across the continent. The Jefferson administration's Louisiana Purchase in 1803 opened the lands west of the Mississippi to federal expansion. Within thirty years, Jefferson's suggestion that the eastern Indians move west had become a national policy of forced removal. The Trail of Tears, the Cherokees' description of their 850-mile march from their lands in northern Georgia to "Indian Territory," in the area of present-day Oklahoma, is a sadly appropriate symbol of that era. Of approximately 16,000 Cherokee people who set out, guarded by U.S. soldiers, more than 4,000 died en route.

Following federal acquisition of the Oregon Territory (1848) and the Southwest, (1846–1848, as a result of the Mexican–American War), California's gold rush and admission to the Union (1850), and the rapid extension of railroads after the Civil War, non-Indian populations surged west across the Mississippi and began to encroach on Indians land throughout the West.

MAP RECONSTRUCTING the topography of Washington in 1791, researched and drawn by architect Don Hawkins. NMAI stands on what is shown here as marshland, where Tiber Creek reaches its southernmost point. Pierre l'Enfant chose the high ground just to the east of that point to be the site of the Capitol.

development. In 1822 Congress formally designated the area between Third and Seventh Streets for the city's use to encourage local commerce and provide income from sales of building lots. Officials added Maine and Missouri Avenues (named for the states most recently added to the Union) parallel to Maryland and Pennsylvania Avenues respectively, thus forming four reservations, designated A, B, C, and D. The city canal and a strip of adjacent park still marked the center of the Mall, but the needs of a growing city dictated the use of the reserved portions for the next century. Hotels, rooming houses, and other commercial establishments characterized the northern streets, while the southern section, separated by the canal from the city center, became more residential and quasi-industrial.

Two major buildings defined the area between Sixth and Seventh Streets. In 1855 Congress built an armory for the city's militia at Seventh Street and what is now Independence Avenue, where the National Air and Space Museum now stands. During the Civil War, the adjoining portion of the Mall became Armory Square Hospital, the first of many military diversions of the area. Another post-war invader, authorized by Congress in 1872, was the Baltimore and Potomac Railroad. Its prominent brick station stood at Sixth Street and what is now Constitution Avenue, the current site of the main building of the National Gallery of Art. Long train sheds stretched southward across the Mall, and the tracks crossed at Sixth Street, passed the Armory, and continued along Maryland Avenue, over the Potomac bridge, and on to Virginia. The railroad was a long-sought improvement, but its location marked a brazen departure from L'Enfant's vision and Mills's and Downing's views of a naturalistic Mall.

NMAI's future site had an especially colorful and long occupational history. After 1849 the coal-gas works and storage tanks of the just-established Washington Gas Light Company gave a semi-industrial flavor to the east end. John Sessford, a statistician who reported annually on Washington's public works for nearly forty years, beginning in the 1820s, noted in 1850, "Very extensive new Gas Works have been erected on square C, near the Canal, and very large pipes laid from them up 4 1/2 street to Pennsylvania avenue, and along the avenue towards the Capitol and President's House. . . ." Gas-lit streets and buildings marked a new era for the city. The gas company's annual report stated that the new works were "not only inviting

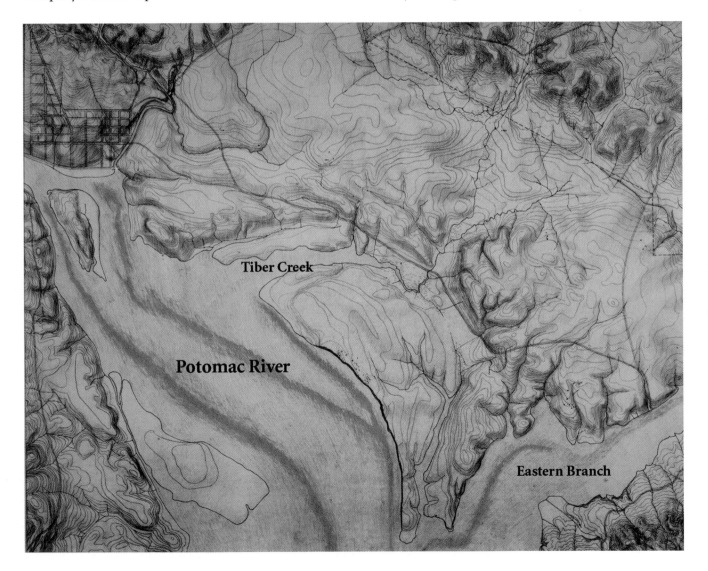

THE MALL from the Capitol, 1870. The temporary buildings of Armory Square Hospital stretch across the Mall from the District Armory Building, beyond the industrial area to left center, where NMAI now stands. Entering the canal from the lower right is what remained of Tiber Creek. The incompleted Washington Monument is faintly visible.

to the eye but are believed to be unsurpassed by any similar works in the country." Beauty, indeed, lay in the eye of the beholder. For several decades, the bulky production plant and tanks contrasted sharply with other structures on the Mall. Eventually, machine shops and an iron foundry joined them, competing visually and functionally with nearby residential and commercial buildings.

The first substantial dwelling on reservation C, now the site of the museum, was the four-story residence of Mary Ann Hall, a single woman who, according to the census of 1840, was living there with several other women. In fact, Hall was operating what became perhaps the most elegant and genteel brothel, or "parlor house," in the city. Records show that

"LIVING AMERICAN INDIANS"

The reform impulse that began to shape the design of the Mall in the late nineteenth century contrasted with the decline of fortunes for American Indians at that time. The 1893 World's Columbian Exposition in Chicago juxtaposed classical cityscapes—the White City—industrial might, and American ingenuity with exhibitions of "Living American Indians" in quaint outdoor settings. The fair's official guide described these exhibitions as showing Indian people "in the exact way their forefathers lived before the white man invaded their lands." The Indians' presence was intended as "back ground to the Exposition," to contrast with 400 years of advances "as shown in the great buildings devoted to the material and educational interests of man."

Beyond the fair, Indians struggled to retain their lands and cultures. The General Allotment Act (1887) called for tribally held land to be given to individuals in 160-acre parcels, with unclaimed or "surplus" land to be sold to fund the establishment of Indian schools. This policy, meant in part to bring Native Americans the full fruits of Euro-American civilization, and other pressures from non-Natives led to the widespread loss of Indian title to reservation lands; forced assimilation into mainstream society, including removal of children to the new government boarding schools; and suppression of Indian ways of life. By the 1900 census, the Indian population of the United States had declined to a low point of 237,196, little more than half the figure of 400,764 recorded by the commissioner of Indian Affairs in 1853. The photography of Edward S. Curtis and James Earle Fraser's widely reproduced sculpture of a defeated Indian horseman, *The End of the Trail,* captured the popular image of American Indians as a "vanishing race." And wealthy New Yorker George Gustav Heye was moved to begin acquiring evidence of what he and others saw as disappearing American Indian cultures.

ALEUTS AT the World's Columbian Exposition, 1893. *Chicago.*

TO BREAK WITH THE PAST

In 1924, moved in part by the patriotism of Indian soldiers during the Great War, Congress extended citizenship to all Indians born in the United States, although as recently as 1948 some states barred Indians from voting. The Indian Reorganization Act and the Johnson–O'Malley Act—the Roosevelt administration's Indian New Deal, enacted in 1934—further reformed federal policy toward Native Americans. The Indian New Deal repealed the General Allotment Act, although not before of two-thirds of formerly Indian-owned land had been lost. Roosevelt's legislation also expanded federal support for tribal governments and for Indian self-determination.

While these acts improved the status of Indians in American society, Native Americans remained marginalized in many ways. On July 8, 1970, in a special message on Indian affairs, President Richard Nixon decried injustices historically visited on American Indians, declaring them "oppressed and brutalized, deprived of their ancestral lands and denied the opportunity to control their own destiny." The time had come, he said, "to break decisively with the past and to create the conditions for a new era in which the Indian future is determined by Indian acts and Indian decisions." Nixon announced a federal policy of Indian self-determination, recognizing historic federal obligations to Indians in return for land and ending the practice of terminating previously instituted federal services to and recognition of Native tribes.

Hall was a steady taxpayer. She left an estate of about $87,000—as much as $2 million in today's currency. In 1886 she was buried in Washington's historic Congressional Cemetery beneath a monument that surely equaled, if not surpassed, those of many of her prominent patrons and guests.

Test digs of the NMAI site done in preparation for the construction of the museum turned up gilt-edged porcelain, bones from fine cuts of meat, and hundreds of champagne corks, leading the Smithsonian's Office of Architectural History and Historic Preservation to support the conclusion that Hall's was a large and prosperous establishment.

During the 1890s, the site was occupied by the Miner Institute for the Education of Colored Youth, and later it became a YMCA for African Americans. The residents of the square block that is now the museum grounds were largely boarders or renters who worked as mechanics, laborers, blacksmiths, painters, brickmakers, seamstresses, shoemakers, chauffeurs, and bartenders. As immigration and urban settlement increased, the perimeter lots were nearly fully occupied, and the alleys housed additional people. German, Irish, Russian, and middle-European immigrants mixed with native-born black and white Americans. Louse Alley, one of the city's most unhealthy and immoral alleys, jammed with overcrowded dwellings, existed within a stone's throw of the Capitol. Finally, no less a personage than Woodrow Wilson's wife, Edith, led the effort to eradicate the evils of alley housing, and in 1914 reform efforts led Congress to enact a citywide ban on houses of prostitution and substandard dwellings. The

MARY ANN HALL'S memorial (foreground). Her mother and two sisters are buried in the family plot, as well. Congressional Cemetery, Washington.

1920 census shows that several buildings once occupied solely by women had been vacated, suggesting that the bawdyhouse ban had an impact. By that time, the population of reservation C was predominantly African American, and included laborers, mechanics, service workers, "a school teacher, and a manicurist." The census records that all of the residents of the twelve-story Vincetta apartment building, constructed on Maryland Avenue in 1905 and one of the tallest in the city, were African Americans.

A MODERN CITY

By the first decades of the twentieth century, many people shared the growing conviction that Washington's emergence as a modern metropolis required the reinstatement of L'Enfant's original plan. The city's lurch into modernization had happened virtually overnight, during the city's brief period of territorial government (1871–1874), when Alexander R. "Boss" Shepherd became the driving force on the powerful Board of Public Works. In three years, Shepherd graded and paved miles of city streets, installed modern sewers

and utilities, filled the city canal to create Constitution Avenue, planted 25,000 trees, and piled up $20 million in debt. In the process, he created perhaps the most modern urban infrastructure in the nation and made Washington instantly credible as an attractive and viable capital. Yet even as the downtown changed, the Mall remained a remote zone.

It took a devastating flood to turn people's attention to the Mall. The flood, in February 1881—not the city's first, but among its most dramatic— drove water through the low-lying areas onto Pennsylvania Avenue and to the foot of Capitol Hill. In response, Congress authorized reclamation of the "Potomac Flats" and installation of protective barriers. Led by Maj. Peter C. Hains, Army engineers spent a decade dredging a channel in the Potomac, filling in the flats and lowlands, installing drainage and hydraulic systems, and building the land barriers that created Hains Point and East and West Potomac Parks along the river. Over the next thirty years, the government spent more than $3 million on reclamation and improvement projects that stretched north from the city's southwest waterfront and Potomac bridge to the foot of the Washington Monument, then west to the mouth of Rock Creek at Georgetown, more than doubling the Mall and related park areas and creating spaces for the Lincoln Memorial, established by Congress in 1911 and dedicated in 1922, and the Kennedy Center, which opened in 1971.

Another critical moment in the Mall's evolution was the World's Columbian Exposition, mounted in Chicago in 1893. Created by planners and architects as a great classical city, the exposition's grand buildings, plazas, and vistas launched the City Beautiful movement and inspired nationwide reforms in municipal design. As the nineteenth century ended, and as prosperity and municipal reform movements grew, both popular opinion and the aesthetics of architects and planners shifted from romanticism toward stately, formal, and uncluttered city design.

TEMPORARY BUILDINGS appear on the Mall as the federal city expands, 1941. By the end of World War II, temporary structures covered NMAI's trapezoidal site and the blocks to its west. Their removal cleared the way for construction of the Hirshhorn Museum (opened in 1974) and the National Air and Space Museum (1976).

L'Enfant's unrealized vision for Washington now seemed both achievable and desirable. It was a time of reflection on the city's history, coupled with anticipation for the century ahead, and politicians and planners seized the moment.

Pressed by the American Institute of Architects, in 1902 James McMillan, senator from Michigan and head of the Senate Committee on the District of Columbia, commissioned a study of the need for a revitalized park system for the area. McMillan assembled a remarkable group, a dream team of figures instrumental in designing the Chicago exposition: Chicago architect Daniel Burnham, who supervised the planning and construction of the fair; Boston landscape designer Frederick Law Olmsted, Jr., most famous today for his role in planning New York's Central Park; architect Charles McKim, whose New York firm McKim, Mead, and White designed the Boston Library, among many iconic projects; and sculptor Augustus Saint-Gaudens, whose works by that time stood in New York, Chicago, and Boston.

The committee was charged with creating a comprehensive plan for the capital's parks and public spaces that would reverse the departures from the L'Enfant plan, recommend places for needed public buildings and monuments, incorporate new parks, provide spaces for health and recreation, and prevent actions detrimental to the "beauty and dignity of the national capital." Titled *Improvement of the Park System of the District of Columbia,* the committee's report was a blueprint that quickly began to transform the Mall and continues to guide planning in the nation's capital.

The committee proposed restoring the vistas west from the Capitol and south from the White House that intersect at the Washington Monument. The new scheme called for clearing the Mall of drives and gardens of trees, removing the picturesque Castle building and

THE 21st-CENTURY Mall, looking west from the 5th-floor terrace of the National Museum of the American Indian to the brick Arts & Industries Building, the Smithsonian Castle, and the Washington Monument. The skyline in the background is in Virginia, across the Potomac River.

THE WETLANDS area to the east of NMAI's entrance reflects the habitat once found along Tiber Creek.

Botanical Gardens, and eliminating the train station and the urban intrusions at the east end of the Mall. It established building sites, terraces, fountains, sculptural settings, and other formal design elements reflective of L'Enfant's vision. Though the plan provoked opposition, over time it achieved its authors' broad aims to unclutter the Mall, formalize its open spaces and building alignments, and provide a template for the acquisition of parklands and the placement of public buildings. The Castle and Botanical Gardens survived, but the trains were relegated to Union Station (1908) in the northeast section of the city, designed by Burnham after he convinced Pennsylvania Railroad magnate Alexander J. Cassatt of the importance of clearing his terminal and tracks from the Mall.

The Smithsonian's National Museum of Natural History (1910) was the first building on the Mall to conform to the committee's projected scale and architectural vision. The National Gallery of Art (1941) and the Museum of History and Technology (1964), now the Museum of American History, arrived later on the north side, followed eventually by the National Gallery's East Building (1978) and sculpture garden (1999). On the south side of the Mall, the Freer Gallery of Art (1923) joined the Smithsonian Castle (1855, though reconstructed and enlarged over the decades) and Arts and Industries Building (1881). To assure adherence to the aesthetic and planning principles of the McMillan Plan, Congress set up the Commission of Fine Arts in 1910 and the National Capital Parks and Planning Commission in 1926.

With the railroad gone, planners next targeted the area immediately west of the Capitol, but things did not go smoothly. For thirty years, factions battled over design, tree removal, buildings and monuments, funding, street locations, and traffic. Temporary buildings erected on the Mall during both world wars blocked development of this prized piece of federal real estate long after World War II ended; the last temporary buildings were not removed until the early 1970s. The projects most crucial to the future NMAI site were the clearing of the Mall between 1934 and 1936, relocation of the Botanical Garden, and development of the Grant Memorial and other designs at the base of Capitol Hill. Most of the buildings on reservation C were gone by 1934, but a World War II office building was then erected and remained standing until the late 1960s.

By 1970 the attention of planners and politicians in Washington turned to designating the use of the wedge-shaped site at the head of the Mall. The sites immediately to the west were committed to the Hirshhorn Museum

(1974) and the National Air and Space Museum (1976), and most informed observers expected that another museum would follow. In the early 1970s—two years before Public Law 94-74, signed on August 8, 1975, stipulated that "the portion of the Mall bounded by Third Street, Maryland Avenue, Fourth Street, and Jefferson Drive in the District of Columbia is reserved as a site for the future public uses of the Smithsonian Institution"—Marvin Sadik, director of the National Portrait Gallery, had pointed out to Smithsonian Secretary S. Dillon Ripley that the "one remaining spot on the Mall might well be devoted to a National Museum of the American Indian." Sadik observed prophetically that the "Museum of the American Indian in New York has splendid stuff, but . . . it does not really give the subject its full due." The apt model, he suggested, was the Museo Anthropologia in Mexico City. Sadik wrote to Ripley that it was "high time that the American Indian was seen primarily on his own terms, rather than solely through the eyes of ethnologists, sociologists, historians, art historians, etc."

Sadik raised the matter informally with other officials, including Vice President Nelson Rockefeller, who informed him that the New York State attorney general had said that there was "no hard and fast rule" stating that the MAI collections could not come to Washington. In December 1975, Rockefeller wrote Sadik saying, "I think your suggestion for a National Museum devoted to the American Indian is excellent and I hope that perhaps with all our combined efforts we can really explore and come to terms with the possibilities of this project." Soon after, Secretary Ripley accompanied Representative Sidney R. Yates, the lead member of the House of Representatives for arts appropriations, on a tour of the collections of the Indian museum's Research Branch in the Bronx.

More than a decade passed before the final assignment of the site. Around 1980 the trustees of the Museum of the American Indian–Heye

Foundation initiated talks with the Smithsonian about the possibility of affiliating with the institution while retaining an independent museum in New York. By late 1987 Smithsonian Secretary Robert McCormick Adams, Senator Daniel Inouye (Hawai'i), and New York State and City leaders, including Senator Daniel Patrick Monyihan and Chase Manhattan Bank President David Rockefeller, were in serious negotiations that eventually led to the establishment of the National Museum of the American Indian.

The legislation that created NMAI, Public Law 101-185, signed November 28, 1989, provided that the Smithsonian operate a museum in the Alexander Hamilton U.S. Custom House in New York City, today's George Gustav Heye Center (opened in 1994); care for the collections in a new Cultural Resources Center in Suitland, Maryland (1998); and build its centerpiece museum on the last site on the National Mall. The act launched a rather new type of cultural museum, to be developed with the direct involvement of Native peoples. It was not a museum produced by others for American Indians, but rather one created by American Indians themselves. It would be a place for Native people to celebrate and share their achievements and aspirations as Americans and citizens of the world.

Now two centuries of evolving national policy toward American Indians have converged with equally long efforts to shape the National Mall as a place for public inspiration and education. The assignment of the last building site on the Mall to the National Museum of the American Indian restores this long-contested ground to a use that respects its distant past and offers it a new role as a site of reconciliation. This piece of land, home to so much change in the last two centuries, is now a Native place again, a center for education and celebration, where Native and non-Native people come together to build a respectful and promising future.

FOLLOWING PAGES: The north side of the National Museum of the American Indian at sunrise. Among the messages architect Johnpaul Jones hopes the newest building on the National Mall will convey is this: "We have been here a long time. We have a deep connection to this place."

Acknowledgments

ON BEHALF OF RICK WEST AND MY COLLEAGUES AT NMAI, I WOULD LIKE TO thank the members of the U.S. Congress, and in particular Senators Daniel Inouye and Ben Nighthorse Campbell (Northern Cheyenne), and the late Senator Daniel Patrick Moynihan, for their dedication to building an Indian museum at the very heart of our nation's capital. A debt of gratitude is also due to Smithsonian Secretaries Robert McCormick Adams, I. Michael Heyman, and Lawrence Small, and to the institution's Board of Regents, for their unwavering support for this museum.

No project of this scope could have been completed without the efforts of virtually every part of the Smithsonian. The Offices of Facilities Engineering and Operations, Safety and Environmental Management, Protection Services, Contracting, Architectural History and Historic Preservation, Human Resources, and Planning, Management, and Budget; the staffs of the Chief Financial Officer, Chief Information Officer, Comptroller, and General Counsel; and the people in the S.I. Libraries, Accessibility Program, and Visitor Information and Associates' Reception Center, particularly, have borne a heavy burden of work for the museum with generosity and good grace. It has been a pleasure for me personally to work with Smithsonian Design Manager Lyn Payton and Project Executives Debra Nauta-Rodriguez and Bill Thomas.

A number of architects, engineers, and designers played key roles in the conception and construction of the museum. Venturi, Scott Brown and Associates did the important work of distilling the museum's initial consultations into *The Way of the People,* the architectural program that helped anchor all that followed. The Polshek Partnership, Tobey + Davis, and the Native American Design Collaborative provided architectural and engineering services for the Cultural Resources Center.

The design of the museum on the National Mall reflects the remarkable talent and dedication of Douglas Cardinal, Johnpaul Jones, Ramona Sakiestewa, Donna House, and Lou Weller, and their colleagues at Douglas Cardinal, Ltd., GBQC, Jones & Jones, SmithGroup, the Native Design Collaborative, EDAW, and Polshek. Artists Arthur Amiotte (Oglala Lakota), Susie Bevins (Inupiat), and Lloyd Kiva New (Cherokee), and herbalist Alma Snell (Crow) offered additional guidance as members of the design team's Native Advisory Group. The U.S. Commission of Fine Arts and the National Capital Planning Commission were instrumental in the development of the site and the museum's architecture. Clark/TMR and its subcontractors translated models and drawings into stone and mortar. I would particularly like to thank Paul Brown, Marc Muller, Jim Klein, and the members of the Smithsonian/Bovis crew (the construction-trailer folks) for their support of the museum and their attention to detail.

For more than two years, Dottie Tiger (Sauk–Fox/Yuchi) provided a warm welcome to visitors who stopped by the small exhibition on the construction site to see what we were building. Former NMAI exhibition designer Evi Oehler, my architectural partner on the museum staff, was an indispensable friend. I am just one of many people who are grateful for her tireless work during the project's lengthy design and construction process and for her valuable contributions to the development of the exhibitions.

As NMAI's Facilities Planning Coordinator, I've witnessed first-hand the commitment and professionalism of my colleagues at the Research Branch, the Heye Center, the Cultural Resources Center, and the museum on the National Mall. Donna Scott, Assistant Director for Administration, and her staff had the enjoyable, but daunting responsibility of managing a growing staff and budget. The Office of Development and External Affairs, led by Elizabeth Duggal and her predecessor John Colonghi, together with the director's staff and many others, worked tirelessly to sustain the level of public and private support necessary to build the museum. Thanks are due to Pablita Abeyta (Navajo), Maggie Bertin, and their colleagues in the Membership, Public Affairs, and Special Events Offices.

The Move Team, led by Scott Merritt, inventoried, packed, and transported the Heye collections from the Bronx to Maryland with great care. At the CRC, Pat Nietfeld, Marian Kaminitz, Ann Drumheller, and the Collections Management, Conservation, and Registration staffs remain conscientious about the cultural and spiritual importance of these objects to Native Americans.

NMAI's Curatorial Resources staff, under Assistant Director Bruce Bernstein, worked with Native communities throughout the America's to develop the exhibitions for the museum on the National Mall. The creative people of the Department of Exhibitions and Public Spaces, led by Kerry Boyd, with the able assistance of Karen Fort and an exceptional group of exhibition managers and specialists, envisioned the curatorial and community research in three dimensions. Batwin + Robin Productions made the wonderful film that orients visitors to the museum. Assistant Director Helen Maynor Scheirbeck (Lumbee) and her Department of Public Programs have embraced the challenge of presenting Native cultures in all their vitality and diversity through performances, lectures and symposia, and educational programs. Associate Director Jim Volkert and the Mall Transition Team coordinated work leading up to the museum's opening with imagination and energy. Assistant Director Jim Pepper Henry (Kaw/Muscogee) and the Community Services Department were instrumental in the development of the museum and play a central role in achieving its mission.

On a smaller scale, this book, too, reflects the contributions of many colleagues. During an extraordinarily busy year, the authors of these essays added another deadline to their calendars. Terence Winch, NMAI Head of Publications, conceived of this project and, with Kevin Mulroy, Vice President and Editor-in-Chief of National Geographic Books, oversaw its evolution. Cheryl Wilson provided the original outline for the Table of Contents. Editor Holly Stewart worked closely with the contributors. Ann Kawasaki handled the administrative nuts and bolts of this project with characteristic good grace. Rebecca Lescaze served as project manager for this book at National Geographic with understanding and good cheer; Art Director Peggy Archambault created the lively and elegant design of these pages.

I would also like to thank the NMAI Office of Photo Services—especially supervisory photographer Cynthia Frankenburg and photographers Ernest Amoroso, Katherine Fogden (Mohawk), Walter Larrimore, and Roger Whiteside—and Photo Archivist Lou Stancari and his staff for their timely assistance. Tanya Thrasher (Cherokee) helped identify images for this book. John Timothy II, Director of the Ataloa Lodge Museum, Bacone College, lent us photographs of Bacone, and Roseanne Spinks, of the Bacone Alumni Association, identified the student with Dick West in the NMAI archival photograph on page 50. Maxwell MacKenzie provided the beautiful architectural photography printed throughout this book.

Finally, the National Museum of the American Indian could not have been built without the leadership of Founding Director W. Richard West, Jr., the commitment of the trustees and members of the museum, the support of foundations and corporations, and the generous contributions of Native and non-Native individuals and communities throughout the Americas.

—D.B.S.

Photo Credits

Images from the Photo Archives of the National Museum of the American Indian are identified where they appear by photograph or negative number; the photographers or collections, when known, are given below. Sources for the remaining photographs are identified here.

Cover & page 1, © Maxwell MacKenzie; 4–5, 6–7, © Roberto Ysáis and National Museum of the American Indian, Smithsonian Institution; 8–9, © James Barker; 10–11, © Roberto Ysáis and National Museum of the American Indian, Smithsonian Institution; 12, 14 © Maxwell MacKenzie; 16,17, sketches by Douglas Cardinal; 18, 20, 21 Cynthia Frankenburg; 25, © Maxwell MacKenzie; 26, Duane Blue Spruce, NMAI; 27, © Maxwell MacKenzie; 28, Frederick Starr Collection; 30, Toba P. Tucker; 34–35, Frank G. Speck; 40–41, Rolf Tietgens; 42, Katherine Fogden, NMAI; 44, courtesy of the West family; 46, 48–49, Bacone College Collection; 53, courtesy of the West family; 60, Carmelo Guadagno, NMAI; 63, Pamela Dewey, NMAI; 64, Katherine Fogden, NMAI; 66, Paul Nicklen, National Geographic; 69, © Maxwell MacKenzie; 70, site plan by Polshek, Toby + Davis, Jones & Jones; 71 Herbert Lotz; 72, © Maxwell MacKenzie; 75, Jeff Geissler, © *Albuquerque Journal;* 76, Medford Taylor, National Geographic; 77, Hayes Patrick Lavis, NMAI; 79, Jim Pepper Henry, NMAI; 81, Jeff Geissler, © *Albuquerque Journal;* 84, 85, © Maxwell MacKenzie; 89, Edward H. Davis; 94, 97, Samuel K. Lothrop; 96, Jesse L. Nusbaum; 100, William F. Stiles; 114, Kenneth C. Miller; 116, 119 Katherine Fogden, NMAI; 119, Katherine Fogden, NMAI; 120, architectural drawing by Polshek, Toby + Davis, Native American Design Collaborative; 122, 125, 126, Gale Ellen Wilson, NMAI; 130, Scott Carroll, NMAI; 131, Katherine Fogden, NMAI; 132, courtesy of Jeffrey Sunday and Herby Kirby; 135, 136, David Heald; 139, Roy Gumpel; 142, David Heald; 142–143, Charles C. Ebbetts, Bettmann/CORBIS; 147, Roy Gumpel; 148, illustration © Tom Coffin; 150, © Maxwell MacKenzie; 152, author's collection; 153, Thomas Smillie, Smithsonian; 154, Bettmann/CORBIS; 157, 160, National Archives; 161, daguerreotype attributed to Jesse Whitehurst; 162, attributed to Mathew Brady; 166, 167, Smithsonian; 171, topographical map by Don Hawkins; 172, Library of Congress; 176, National Capital Planning Commission; 177, Association for the Preservation of Historic Congressional Cemetery; 178, © Maxwell MacKenzie; 181, Wood Ronsaville Harlin, Inc., © Smithsonian Institution; 184–185, © Maxwell MacKenzie; back cover, Kasota stone © Maxwell MacKenzie, inset attributed to Fred Harvey.

NMAI object photography
Page 38, David Heald; 42, Katherine Fogden; 47, R. A. Whiteside; 54, 56–57, 78, David Heald; 82, NMAI Move Team; 91, David Heald; 105–108, Ernest Amoroso; 112, 137, Katherine Fogden; 144, David Heald.

Contributors

Duane Blue Spruce (Laguna and San Juan Pueblo), a licensed architect and member of the American Indian Council of Architects and Engineers, served as primary design and construction liaison between NMAI and the architectural design team for the museum on the National Mall. He played the same role in the design and construction of NMAI's Cultural Resources Center. Before coming to the museum in 1993, Duane was assistant project manager of the Institute of American Indian Arts in Santa Fe.

Douglas E. Evelyn, deputy director of NMAI, did his doctoral dissertation on the architectural history of the Patent Office Building, now home of the Smithsonian American Art Museum and the National Portrait Gallery. His research interests include Washington's history as a national capital, and the development of national museums and exhibitions as instruments of American democracy. He has been treasurer of the American Association of Museums, president of the American Association of State and Local History, and manager of the Papers of Robert Mills, the most significant American-born architect of the early nineteenth century. Doug's book *On this Spot: Pinpointing the Past in Washington, D.C.,* co-authored with Paul Dickson, is a local bestseller.

John Haworth (Cherokee) is assistant deputy director of NMAI and director of the museum's George Gustav Heye Center in New York. He currently sits on the boards of Americans for the Arts, the Exhibition Alliance, and the Lower Manhattan Cultural Council. Before joining the museum staff in 1995, John served as assistant commissioner for cultural institutions at the New York City Department of Cultural Affairs, where he also worked with education programs.

George P. Horse Capture (A'aninin), has been with the museum since 1994, and holds the title special assistant and senior counselor to the director. He is the author of *Powwow* and, with his son Joseph D. Horse Capture, of *Beauty, Honor, and Tradition: The Legacy of Plains Indian Shirts,* and has contributed essays to many other publications. Before joining NMAI, George taught at the college level and worked as curator at the Plains Indian Museum in Cody, Wyoming.

Liz Hill (Red Lake Band of Chippewa) is a writer, radio producer, and public relations consultant based in Washington, D.C. In 2001, her news writing was honored by the Native American Journalists Association. Liz was NMAI's director of public affairs from 1996 to 1997.

Donna House (Navajo/Oneida) is a botanist and ethnobotanist with particular interests in indigenous ecological knowledge and environmental issues. She works as a consultant and researcher to identify culturally important and rare native plants and find ways to protect their habitats. Earlier in her career, she worked for The Nature Conservancy as a scientist and director of the Navajo Nation Heritage Program. She also served as a Plant Recover Team member for the U.S. Fish and Wildlife Service. Donna inhabits a farm along the Rio Grande in northern New Mexico.

Johnpaul Jones (Cherokee/Choctaw) is founding principal of Jones & Jones, Architects and Landscape Architects, based in Seattle, Washington. Born in Okmulgee, Oklahoma, he has worked closely with Native American tribes throughout the United States to incorporate their architectural and cultural heritage into his designs. His work on nature parks, interpretive parks, and many other projects has won recognition for heightening human sensitivity to cultural and environmental issues.

Mary Jane Lenz has been a member of NMAI's Cultural Resources Department since the museum's inception in 1989. Before that, she was a curator at the Museum of the American Indian–Heye Foundation in New York. In fact, her association with the Heye collections dates to 1975, when she was a volunteer at the museum. Most recently, Mary Jane curated the exhibition *Many Hands, Many Voices: Window on Collections* for the new museum on the National Mall. Her book *Small Spirits: Native American Dolls from the National Museum of the American Indian* was published in 2004.

Ramona Sakiestewa (Hopi) is best known for her textile art, although she is also an accomplished painter, monotype printmaker, and designer. Her tapestries—inspired by Modern art and the cultural traditions of places she has traveled, as well as by Pueblo weaving—appear in numerous museums and collections. A former chair of the New Mexico Arts Commission, Ramona heads the Board of Directors of the Santa Fe Art Institute. She lives in Santa Fe in a house she designed with her husband, architect Andrew Merriell. Her son, Micah Sakiestewa-Sze, is a chemical engineer and ceramist.

W. Richard West, Jr. (Southern Cheyenne and member of the Cheyenne and Arapaho Tribes of Oklahoma), has devoted his career to working with American Indians on cultural, educational, legal, and governmental issues. Before his appointment as Director of NMAI, he practiced law, representing numerous Indian tribes and organizations before federal, state, and tribal courts, executive departments of the federal government, and Congress. Since joining NMAI, he has been active in the American Association of Museums, where he served as chair from 1998 to 2000. Rick and his wife, Mary Beth, have two adult children, Amy and Ben.

Authors' Notes

Foreword, pp. 15–29

pp. 19–21

Quotations from participants in the museum's early consultations are from the Introduction to *The Way of the People,* volume 1. Speakers are not identified. *The Way of the People* is a detailed architectural program produced for the National Museum of the American Indian and Smithsonian's Office of Design and Construction by Venturi, Scott Brown and Associates, Architects, between 1991 and 1993.

Introduction, pp. 31–43

This essay has been adapted and expanded from George Horse Capture's Preamble to volume 2 of *The Way of the People.*

Chapter 1, pp. 44–65

p. 65

Poem: Simon J. Ortiz, "It Doesn't End, of Course." In *Woven Stone,* p. 147. Tucson: University of Arizona Press, 1992.

Chapter 3, pp. 86–115

p. 87

"His museum is his monument": J. Alden Mason, "George G. Heye, 1874–1957." Leaflets of the Museum of the American Indian, Heye Foundation, 6, 1959.

p. 89

"I obtained a number of Navaho Indians for use as laborers . . .": Kevin Wallace, "A Reporter at Large: Slim-Shin's Monument." *The New Yorker,* 36 (19 November 1960), pp. 104–146.

pp. 90–91

"Mr. Heye has become greatly interested . . .": Letter from George Pepper, NMAI Archives, box OC 87, folder 8.

p. 93

Marshall Saville's report: The George G. Heye Expedition: Contributions to South American Archeology. Vol. 1: *The Antiquities of Manabi, Ecuador: A Preliminary Report,* New York: Irving Press, 1907. Vol. 2: *The Antiquities of Manabi, Ecuador: Final Report,* New York: Irving Press, 1910.

p. 94

Heye's divorce settlement: Wallace, *The New Yorker.*

p. 98

Remarks from the dinner at the Lotos Club: Museum of the American Indian–Heye Foundation (MAI–HF) Annual Report, April 1, 1922–April 1, 1923, p. 2. "The complete design of these doors . . .": Letter from Berthold Neber, NMAI Archives, box A–122 U79, folder 20.

p. 103

John Williams's suggested anniversary donation: Letter from Heye to Joseph Keppler, NMAI Archives, box V–K, folder F–4A.

p. 104

Accomplishments during 1924: MAI–HF Annual Report, 1924–25.

p. 105

Discarded barrels of potsherds: Samuel K. Lothrop, "George Gustav Heye —1874–1956 [sic]" *American Antiquity,* vol. 23 (1957–58), p. 67. Heye's "Golden Rule": Notes by Donald Cadzow, NMAI Archives, box OC 124, folder 22.

p. 106

"Right now I have quite a few specimens . . .": Letter to Julius Carlebach, NMAI Archives, box VA, folder 10.

p. 107

Heye's purchases from curio shops: Kate C. Duncan, *1001 Curious Things: Ye Olde Curiosity Shop and Native American Art.* Seattle: University of Washington Press, 2000. p. 94.

pp. 107–08

"As the Indians felt . . .": MAI–HF Annual Report, 1922–23, p. 4.

p. 110

"I will do anything . . .": Letter to C. B. Moore, NMAI Archives, box OC 121, folder 1D. "wreck of the archaeological department": H. Newell Wardle, "Wreck of the Archeological Department of the Academy of the Natural Sciences of Philadelphia" *Science,* vol. 70. pp. 119–121. "This little lady . . .": Unpublished transcript by E. K. Burnett, NMAI Archives, box V–W, folder 13, p. 17.

p. 112

". . . Solely for the purpose . . .": MAI–HF Annual Report, 1937–38, p. 4.

Heye's nicknames: Edmund Carpenter, "Repatriation." *European Review of Native American Studies,* vol. 15:1 (2001), p. 12.

Chapter 4, pp. 116—31

Quotations throughout the chapter are from the author's interviews.

Chapter 5, pp. 132–49

p. 137

"the costliest visit . . .": William Grimes, "The Indian Museum's Last Stand." New York Times, Nov. 27, 1988, p. 76.

p. 140

"Nice place to visit . . .": Stan Freberg, *The United States of America, vol. 1, The Early Years.* "Sale of Manhattan." New York: Capitol Records, 1961.

p. 141

"[T]he settlement which certain Indians permitted . . .": Reginald Pelham Bolton, *Indians in Possession of New York.* Indian Notes and Monographs, vol. 2, no. 7. New York: Heye Foundation, 1920, p. 237.

p. 149

Coyote story and quotations: Mary Kreipe de Montaño, and Tom Coffin, *Coyote in Love with a Star.* Washington & New York: NMAI & Abbeville. 1998.

Chapter 6, pp. 150–83

p. 154

Natives lived throughout the area: Robert L. Humphrey and Mary Elizabeth Chambers, *Ancient Washington: American Indian Cultures of the Potomac Valley*, Washington Studies, no. 6, ii. Washington: George Washington University, January 1977. pp. 22–31.

p. 155

"Mr. Carroll's part of Dudington Pasture": Allen C. Clark, "Origin of the Federal City," *Records of the Columbia Historical Society (RCHS)*, vol. 35–36. Washington: Columbia Historical Society, 1935. Plate 5, pp. 85, 94.

pp. 155–56

Jefferson's efforts " . . . to save the union": Thomas Jefferson note on the Residence Bill, ca. May 1790. In Saul K. Padover, ed., *Thomas Jefferson and the National Capital, 1783–1818.* Washington: U.S. Government Printing Office, 1946, pp. 11–12; quote, note 3.

p. 156

Agreement on the compromise and the Residence Bill: Jefferson note in Padover.

pp. 156–57

L'Enfant's relationship with Washington: H. Paul Caemmerer, *The Life of Pierre Charles L'Enfant.* Washington: National Republic, 1950. pp. 25, 43–46, 52, 57, 61, 127, 103–109, 127–129; quote, p. 66. Also, Padover, pp. 42–43.

p. 158

"Jenkins Heights . . ." and a "Grand Avenue": Caemmerer, pp. 152, 1

p. 159

"On the east side of the road . . ." and "a complete little wilderness": Christian Hines, *Early Recollections of Washington City.* Washington: Junior League (reprint). September 1866. pp. 7, 10.

p. 159–60

Latrobe's description of the Mall: Edward C. Carter II, John C. Van Horne, and Lee W. Formwalt, eds., *Journals of Benjamin Henry Latrobe, 1799–1820*, vol. 3. New Haven and London: Yale, 1980. p. 70.

p. 160

"Washington has lately been deprived . . .": David Baillie Warden, *A Chorographical and Statistical Description of the District of Columbia.* Paris: Smith, Rue Montmorency, 1816. p. 60.

p. 160–61

Efforts to tame Tiber Creek: Cornelius W. Heine, "The Washington City Canal," *RCHS*, vol. 53–56 (1959). pp. 1–27; quote, p. 21. Robert Mills, Petition to House and Senate, c. 1852. See also Pamela Scott, ed., *The Papers of Robert Mills, 1781–1855.* Wilmington: Scholarly Resources, 1990. Microform 2950.

p. 161–62

Law's proposed botanical garden: Thomas Law, untitled manuscript, Peter Force Collection, Library of Congress,. (undated, ca. 1805). Microfilm reel 12.

p. 165

For more on Mills and the museum in the Patent Office Building, see Douglas E. Evelyn, "The Washington Years: The U.S. Patent Office," in John M. Bryan, ed., *Robert Mills, Architect.* Washington: American Institute of Architects, 1989. The primacy of Thomas McKenny's museum is from conversations with Herman J. Viola, author of *The Indian Legacy of Charles Bird King.* Washington: Smithsonian, 1976.

pp. 167–68

Mills's plan: Robert Mills to Joel R. Poinsett, February 23, 1841. See

Scott, *Papers of Robert Mills*, Microform 2179. Poinsett was Secretary of War in the Van Buren administration. He was also an amateur botanist. As the nation's first ambassador to Mexico in the 1820s, he had introduced the poinsettia to the United States and was its namesake. Mills's plan for the Mall and other early plans and precedents are discussed in Pamela Scott's "'This Vast Empire': The Iconography of the Mall, 1791–1848," in Richard Longstreth, ed., *The Mall in Washington, 1791–1991*. Washington: National Gallery of Art, 1991, rev. 2002. pp. 37–58.

p. 168
Downing's plan: Therese O'Malley, "'A Public Museum of Trees': Mid-19th-Century Plans for the Mall," Longstreth, ed., *The Mall in Washington*, pp. 61

p. 169
The Trail of Tears: Duane Champagne, ed., *Chronology of Native North American History*. Detroit, Washington, London: Gale Research, 1994. pp. 148–149.

pp. 171–172
Industrial history of the NMAI site: John Sessford, "The Sessford Annals, 1822–1859," *RCHS*, vol. 11. Washington: Columbia Historical Society, 1908; quote, p. 350; Albert W. Atwood, ed., Robert R. Hershman and Edward T. Stafford, preparers, *Growing with Washington*. Washington: Washington Gas Light Company, 1948. p. 35.

pp. 172–74
Demographics of the NMAI site: Smithsonian website www.si.edu/oahp/nmaidig/start.htm, Archaeological Investigations, National Museum of the American Indian Site, Washington, D.C. pp. 4, 5, 8–10. The website is based on John Milner Associates, Phase II Evaluative Testing, National Museum of the American Indian, Mall Museum Site, Washington, D.C., ODC project 902003, June 7, 1996. The full report is located in the Washingtoniana Division of the Martin Luther King Memorial Library. Report was prepared by Donna J. Seifert. For occupational histories, see Appendix 1.

p. 173
Sources for "Living American Indians": For 1893 fair exhibits, see John J. Flinn, *Official Guide to the World's Columbian Exposition*. Chicago: The Columbian Guide Company, 1893. pp. 54–55. For 1900 census data, Champagne, p. 241; 1853 data, J. D. B. DeBow, *Statistical View of the United States, Compendium of the Seventh Census*.

Washington: A.O.P. Nicholson, Public Printer, 1854. p. 191 DeBow sets the Indian population in 1853 at 400,764, including 271,930 in California, Oregon, and Texas, etc., that is, areas added since 1828.

p. 174
Sources for "To Break with the Past": Champagne, *Chronology*. 1930s, pp. 237, 283, 293; Nixon, p. 377; quote, p. 521.

pp. 175–77
Boss Shepherd: Fremont Rider, *Rider's Washington* (New York: The Macmillan Company, 1924), xxxiv–xxxv.

p. 177
The $3.4–million cost of the reclamation: Gordon Chappell, *Historic Resource Study, East and West Potomac Parks: A History*. Denver: National Park Service, June 1973. Appendix A.

p. 179–80
The McMillan plan: Charles Moore, ed., *The Improvement of the Park System of the District of Columbia*. Washington: GPO, 1902. pp. 10–11.

pp. 182–83
Creating NMAI: For memoranda from Marvin Sadik to Robert A. Brooks (24 April 1973), and to S. Dillon Ripley (4 May 1973), see Smithsonian Archives, record unit 426, National Portrait Gallery, and director's records, box 10, American Indian, Museum (1973–80). For Nelson Rockefeller to Sadik (23 January 1976), see Sadik, personal correspondence in Douglas E. Evelyn's "Native Place" research file, NMAI Archives, Cultural Resources Center, Suitland, Maryland. See also Evelyn's memos in research file of interviews of Sadik and former Smithsonian legislative liaison Margaret C. Gaynor.

Back cover

Quotation: Paul Chaat Smith, "Season of Struggle." In *Native Universe: Voices of Indian America*, ed. Gerald McMaster and Clifford E. Trafzer. Washington: NMAI and National Geographic, 2004. p. 184.

Photograph: Hopi Boy, 1914. *Walpi, Arizona*. T6104.

Spirit of a Native Place

BUILDING THE NATIONAL MUSEUM OF THE AMERICAN INDIAN

Edited by
Duane Blue Spruce

PUBLISHED BY
THE NATIONAL GEOGRAPHIC SOCIETY
IN ASSOCIATION WITH THE NATIONAL
MUSEUM OF THE AMERICAN INDIAN

John M. Fahey, Jr., President
and Chief Executive Officer

Gilbert M. Grosvenor, Chairman of the Board

Nina D. Hoffman, Executive Vice President

PREPARED BY THE BOOK DIVISION

Kevin Mulroy, Vice President and Editor-in-Chief

Charles Kogod, Illustrations Director

Marianne R. Koszorus, Design Director

STAFF FOR THIS BOOK

Rebecca Lescaze, Project Editor

Peggy Archambault, Art Director

Meredith Wilcox, Illustrations Assistant

R. Gary Colbert, Production Director

Richard S. Wain, Production Project Manager

Cameron Zotter, Design Assistant

MANUFACTURING AND QUALITY CONTROL

Christopher A. Liedel, Chief Financial Officer

Phillip L. Schlosser, Managing Director

John T. Dunn, Technical Director

Vincent P. Ryan, Manager

Clifton M. Brown, Manager

NATIONAL GEOGRAPHIC

One of the world's largest nonprofit scientific and educational organizations, the National Geographic Society was founded in 1888 "for the increase and diffusion of geographic knowledge." Fulfilling this mission, the Society educates and inspires millions every day through its magazines, books, television programs, videos, maps and atlases, research grants, the National Geographic Bee, teacher workshops, and innovative classroom materials. The Society is supported through membership dues, charitable gifts, and income from the sale of its educational products. This support is vital to National Geographic's mission to increase global understanding and promote conservation of our planet through exploration, research, and education.

For more information, please call 1-800-NGS LINE (647-5463) or write to the following address: National Geographic Society, 1145 17th Street N.W., Washington, D.C. 20036-4688 U.S.A. Visit the Society's Web site at www.nationalgeographic.com.

Smithsonian
National Museum of the American Indian

Published in conjunction with the opening of the new museum on the National Mall of the Smithsonian's National Museum of the American Indian, Washington, D.C., September 21, 2004.

Head of Publications, NMAI: Terence Winch
Project Editor, NMAI: Holly Stewart

The Smithsonian's National Museum of the American Indian is dedicated to working in collaboration with the indigenous peoples of the Americas to protect and foster Native cultures throughout the Western Hemisphere. The museum's publishing program seeks to augment awareness of Native American beliefs and lifeways, and to educate the public about the history and significance of Native cultures.

For information about the Smithsonian's National Museum of the American Indian, visit the NMAI Website at www.AmericanIndian.si.edu.

Library of Congress Cataloging-in-Publication Data
Spirit of a Native place : building the National Museum of the American Indian /
Duane Blue Spruce, editor.
    p. cm.
  ISBN 0-7922-8214-0
1. National Museum of the American Indian (U.S.)--History. 2. National Museum of the American Indian (U.S.). George Gustave Heye Center--History. 3. National Museum of the American Indian (U.S.)--Buildings. 4. National Museum of the American Indian (U.S.). George Gustave Heye Center--Buildings. 5. Indians of North America--Museums--Washington (D.C.). 6. Indians of North America--Museums--New York (State)--New York. 7. Ethnological museums and collections--Washington (D.C.) 8. Ethnological museums and collections--New York (State) N.Y. 9. Washington (D.C.)--Buildings, structures. 10. New York (N.Y.)--Buildings, structures. I. Blue Spruce, Duane. II. National Museum of the American Indian (U.S.)
  E76.86.W182N377 2004
  973.04'97'0074753--dc22
                                        2004054691